IN MY STEPS

Bob Clapp

abbott press®
A DIVISION OF WRITER'S DIGEST

Abbott Press books may be ordered through booksellers or by contacting:

Abbott Press
1663 Liberty Drive
Bloomington, IN 47403
www.abbottpress.com
Phone: 1-866-697-5310

ISBN: 978-1-4582-0869-9 (sc)
ISBN: 978-1-4582-0868-2 (e)

Library of Congress Control Number: 2013905652

Printed in the United States of America.

Abbott Press rev. date: 3/26/2013

TABLE OF CONTENTS

PREFACE

You don't have to agree with everything you read in a book (except the Bible). Although you can't argue with experience, almost every teaching bouncing around in the churches today is argued and debated. There are many differences among God's people. There are a variety of views on the 2nd coming of Jesus, baptism, speaking in tongues, the baptism of the Holy Spirit, which is the true Lord's Day, etc. Romans 14 makes it clear that many of our differences are acceptable and we have to respect and honor one another and agree to disagree. Hebrews 8 also makes it clear that we "shall all be taught of God" and that He will write His laws for each of us on our heart and mind.

Our thoughts and ways are not God's ways and thoughts. "All we like sheep have gone astray and turned every one to his own way." Isa. 53:6. We are a fallen people living in a fallen world. Don't expect perfection from anyone's book or life but your Savior and His word. Although I confess to be a fallen human being I've done my best to be as honest, sincere and genuine as I can in sharing the life I've thus far lived on planet earth. I've sought to evaluate what God has done in, around, through and for me over the years. I hope it encourages, comforts, challenges and builds you up.

I read somewhere that the old-time sower when sowing his fields would fill his bag not only with good seed, but a fair amount of dirt. As he reached in the bag for a handful of seed to scatter he would bring out some dirt as well. As he scattered the good seed, the extra dirt kept him from sowing it too thick and thus choking it back from greater fruitfulness. There may be some "dirt" in what I have written. Simply set on the shelf what you disagree with or find difficult. Embrace what is good and be blessed.

INTRODUCTION

Years ago I read the book "In His Steps" by Charles Sheldon. It was good and inspiring at the time. It's the story of how several men determined to live each day in the manner they thought Jesus would live. I have learned over the years that the book came up short of the real Christian dynamic. In the first place I can't live as Jesus lived. I'm not God and He is. As Isaiah said "I'm an unclean man in the midst of an unclean people." But I have invited Jesus to come and live in my heart. I believe He does. He says in Rev 3:20 "Behold I stand at the door and knock. If any man hear my voice and open the door, I will come in." Throughout the New Testament Scriptures we read of how we are being conformed to the image of Jesus; that He is living His life in us more and more as we surrender more and more to Him. It is in this understanding that I have written "In My Steps." He wants to live His life in me. He is doing that as much as I believe and let Him and that grows with each passing year. We need to change WWJD (What Would Jesus Do) to WIJD (What Is Jesus Doing). That is the real dynamic of the Christian life. As someone has said "be patient with me, God isn't through with me yet." Also someone said "I'm not what I ought to be, but I'm a long ways from what I used to be." We are all being processed into vessels of His life. That is what this book is all about . . . Jesus walking "In My Steps." He is living His life in us as we trust and surrender to Him. He is loving through our hearts, working through our hands, and walking in our feet. I hope as you read this book you will see how Jesus has progressively increased His presence in me over the years in order to manifest and magnify Himself through me. (Phil. 1:20, 21) Lead on oh King Eternal.

All Scripture quotations are taken from the New King James Version.

PART ONE

*My early years from
birth to 2nd birth*

FROM INFANCY TO MY TEENS

My first introduction to Jesus came from my mother. She was a woman of great faith, humility and love. She was well respected in our community as a woman of God. All of us six kids were taught the stories from the Bible. She would pray with us every night as she tucked us into bed. During the day we would often hear her singing a hymn, sometimes it was in rhythm to the old wringer washing machine.

Mom did not have an easy life. She was married to a man 16 years her senior and he certainly wasn't the easiest man to live with. In spite of their many differences and difficulties they celebrated over 50 years of marriage. Mom grew up in Arkansas with her 8 siblings. She had 4 brothers and 4 sisters. Her dad sexually abused the 5 girls. As a result most of them left home at an early age. Mom was 17 when she married dad and she had only known him for two weeks. Apparently she seized the opportunity to get away from a dysfunctional home.

Dad grew up in central Illinois in a farming family along with his two brothers and two sisters. Dad didn't take to farming, but loved hunting, trapping, fishing and the great outdoors. That caused conflicts with his folks who wanted their boys to be active in agriculture. At one time his mother even had his older brother take his much loved hunting dogs out and shoot them. Like mom, his home life was such that he also left home at an early age. After two failed marriages and at the age of 33 he ended up in the middle of Arkansas where he met, wooed and won the hand of mom in marriage. They came back to Illinois to make their life together.

It was the years of the Great Depression and because of the hard times they lived for awhile with grandpa and grandma. While living there my two older brothers were born. Sometime before I was born they had moved a couple of miles NW of Oakland back in the woods. My mom shot squirrels off the roof to add to the meals. Dad continued the rest of his life deeply in love with hunting and trapping and some years he made his living from his quarry. He also worked hard as a mechanic. The depression put the squeeze on lots of folks and they were no exception. When mom told dad that she was pregnant with me he had four words for her: "Get rid of it."

Ever the faithful and obedient wife she tried. Abortions were not the easy fix in the 30's that they are today. She tried all the tricks of the time to no avail. I guess I refused to die, or more accurately, God kept me alive. She felt terrible that she had tried to kill me. Forty years later she told me of that experience. "I felt like you were no longer my son. Since I had given you up, I believed God had taken you up, and I knew from that day forward you belonged to Him in some special way." The Scripture in Psalms 27:10 seems so appropriate ""When my father and my mother forsake me, then the Lord will take care of me."[1] I knew nothing of her commitment when years later I felt the calling of God on my life to preach, but now I understand. Jeremiah's words in Jer.1:5 became real to me: "Before I formed you in the womb I knew you; before you were born I sanctified you; I ordained you a prophet to the nations."

I have no memory of living in the country. When I was two we moved into town to a house on the North side of Oakland on a dead-end street. Over the next 10 years 3 more siblings were born, two boys and one girl. Although we bordered on poverty we were a happy bunch and hardly noticed the inconveniences. We boys followed in dad's footsteps and brought rabbits, squirrels, quail, pheasants and fish to the dinner table. However, in spite of mom's attendance to our spiritual growth we often indulged in our share of misbehaviors.

---

[1] New King James Version and so with all quotations in this book unless otherwise noted.

A cousin took me and a neighbor girl under the house and taught us the pleasures of sex before we reached school age. Such promiscuity became all too common over the ensuing years as me and a brother "played" with a neighbor girl almost every day. Again God stepped in and brought an end to our behavior as we neared puberty. Those were the days before TV and every night we listened to an old radio after we had gone to bed and turned the lights out. One night there was a program about venereal disease among young people. If it was meant to scare kids out of promiscuity it worked. I wonder if the neighbor girl ever figured out why we suddenly stopped coming around to see her. We went for several days scared out of our wits, believing we were either going to die or go insane from our misbehavior. Finally one day my brother got the courage to ask mom what venereal disease was. I don't know to this day what all she said, but I walked away confident we were okay. If she had known what we had been up to she might have talked a different story, especially since one girl did end up with syphilis shortly after.

Perhaps it was the withdrawal from sex with the neighbor girl that led to my next sexual sin. A school-mate seduced me into a homosexual act. Again I believe God stepped in and caused a couple of things that kept me from pursuing that life-style and sin. First of all we did not come to a climax, but there was enough pleasure that I sought to do the same with another class-mate that I thought might be interested. I was wrong and he laughed me to scorn. The deep embarrassment of that experience put and end to any more desire in that direction. Homosexuality is a sin. The Bible condemns it. God calls it an abomination. "If a man lies with a male as he lies with a woman, both of them have committed an abomination. They shall surely be put to death. Their blood shall be upon them" Levi. 20:13. Just because we feel a desire for something does not define who we are. We are a fallen race and during a life-time we will feel lots of strong desires that are not right. God warned Israel about "intense craving" back in Num. 10:4 "Now the mixed multitude who were among them yielded to *intense craving*." Wrong is wrong no matter how much you may crave it. Right is right no matter how little interest you have in it. As fallen creatures we need our standards to be set by our Creator, not by our desires and interests or the pressures of a perverted fallen society.

Mom dressed us up and marched us off to Sunday school and church every Sunday at the local Christian church. We learned right from wrong and that Jesus was more than a baby in a manger. We all learned that the ways of God were worth pursuing and we all became believers in Jesus Christ in due season. One Sunday during my junior year I walked the aisle, took the preacher's hand, repeated the sinner's prayer and was baptized. Although I don't believe I was saved on that occasion, it did put a desire in me to seek the Lord and His will for my life. It would be another seven years before I would make the surrender that saves. But I was started in the right direction.

Shortly after that experience we celebrated the Junior/Senior prom. I was a junior at the time. A half dozen of us boys didn't have dates. After the meal we left the dance and took off for a nearby town to pick up some alcohol. We picked out the oldest looking guy to go in and buy us a bottle. I was sitting by the window in the front seat on the passenger side. As the bottle passed across the back it was handed up to me and I passed it to the guy in the middle without taking a drink.

"Hey Bob, aren't you drinking?" he asked.

"Nope" I replied.

"Why not?" they all echoed.

"I joined the church last Sunday and I don't think I should."

The guy in the middle said "Well if you're not, neither am I" and he passed the bottle to the driver. "Well if you two aren't, then I'm not either" and he passed the bottle to the back. Of the six guys in the car only one ended up drinking that night. Isn't it amazing how one person's example can set the stage to help others?

A little later we were in the country flying down a gravel road that we were not familiar with. Suddenly we came upon an unexpected corner. We were going too fast and in an attempt to make the curve the car slid sideways in the gravel, hit a dead-furrow and slowly began to roll over. I was looking out the window as I saw the dirt field coming up to meet me, and I cried out "Jesus Christ." That had been my favorite cuss word up to that time. I don't know to this day if I was cussing or praying, but I made up my mind that after that I would only use that name in praise and prayer from henceforth. As we climbed out of the car, tipped on its side, the one guy who had continued to drink took the bottle and threw it as far as he could into the field as he yelled out "This is the cause of it all."

Although drunkenness is condemned in the Bible, I cannot say that it condemns drinking in moderation. I cannot drink because it is written on my heart to abstain. It is a respect for my mother as much as a respect for God and my neighbor, but I don't throw stones at anyone who "socially drinks." That's between you and God.

I learned another good lesson during my high school years. I was very active in the Scouting program and had worked my way through the Cub Scouts, Boy Scouts, and Explorer Scouts and eventually even became a Scoutmaster. I loved the hikes, camp-outs and camaraderie of my peers. My high school principal called me into his office one day. "Bob, the Lion's club came to me and told me they would like to send you to the Philmont Scout Ranch." Philmont is the premier scout ranch of scouting. He built me up good with the idea. Then he lowered the boom: "But I told them 'no way' because you are nothing but trouble around this school." If he thought I was trouble before, I walked out of that office with the bitter determination to be more trouble. I think he blew a golden opportunity. I think if he had said "I'm going to give you a chance. If you will stay out of trouble and get your grades up, I'll give my consent for them to send you." I think I would have busted my buttons to do just that. Over the years I've tried to do that with young people I've worked with. I learned a valuable lesson.

My pastor was also my Scoutmaster and he was instrumental in helping me live out my conscience toward God. He was the one that led me into baptism. He instilled in me a desire to preach. He took me and others to senior day at a Bible college and I developed a desire to go there. One doesn't remember too many sermons that he hears in a life-time, but I'll never forget the message I heard in chapel that day at college. One of the professors spoke on "How to fail successfully." The gist of what he said was "if you want to be a success in the eyes of God you will be a failure in the eyes of man. If you want to be a success in the eyes of men you will probably be a failure in the eyes of God." I took that message to heart that day and have tried to live by it ever since. It is far more important to me that I please God than that I please men. I have found it's the best way to live.

OFF TO COLLEGE AND MARRIAGE

During our senior year me and my girl-friend began dating. The sexual desires aroused in my younger years came back with a roar and all too soon we were pregnant. Back in the 50's the only course acceptable was to have a "shot-gun-wedding" and we were wed a couple of months after I had started Bible College. We found a small trailer on campus, purchased it, moved in and began a marriage that has continued nearly 60 years although with lots of ups and downs. We have a lot of fond memories of those 3 years of living on campus in that trailer court full of fellow believers. I got a job working for the school and although finances were tight we were living a happy life as two children entered our lives in the crowded little trailer. I loved the college environment and pulled mostly "A's" as opposed to the "C's" of high school.

It was interesting what $1.00 would buy back in those days. Time and again a friend or relative would send us a needed dollar in the mail. I would walk to a nearby grocery store and come home with a gallon of milk, a loaf of bread, a package of hot dogs, and a bunch of carrots. I bought all that for a dollar and it would feed us for several days. I don't think you could buy any one of those items for a dollar today.

Many of us went out on week-ends to preach in churches. I began preaching in a very small church right in town, but soon I began traveling 200 miles every other week-end to a church in northern Missouri. Me and another preacher who was preaching near there shared our traveling expenses. Life was looking good.

Several of us students began having street meetings every Friday night downtown along tavern row. We took a pick-up truck, put a piano in it, did some singing and praying and then one of us would climb on top of the piano to preach while others would go into the taverns and invite folks out to come and listen. The endeavor grew. We had upwards of 70 students showing up to minister. It was getting late in the fall so we began looking for a place to get inside. We found an empty store building and the first night there we took up enough money to pay the first month's rent. We felt the school might not like our little out-reach so we figured we better get organized so we could give them reasonable answer if we got called in and questioned. We elected 7 guys to put together our organization. I was one of the seven.

After that Friday night meeting I left for Missouri the next morning and was out of the circle of things until Monday evening. In the middle of the afternoon on Monday one of the seven guys walked up on the job where I was working on the school and he was crying. "What's the matter George, why are you crying?"

"Haven't they caught you yet?"

"Hasn't who caught me yet, what are you talking about?"

"The president and some of the faculty have been catching each of the seven guys one by one and drilling them."

"Surely they haven't caught Given yet?" Given was the one who had started the Friday night meetings. I knew he was strong in will and determination and not easily turned from what he believed.

"They have him in the office right now."

I threw down my tools and ran to the trailer, grabbed my Bible and hurried back to the office. I got there just as my dear brother was coming out along with adults who had been grilling him.

"You're not giving up the street meetings are you?" I asked him.

"I don't know" he choked out between tears and sobs. I've never seen what happens to a person who has been "brain-washed" but I think that was what I witnessed in that hallway that day.

Strange thing is they never did call me in. I guess they figured I was a hopeless case and it would have been a waste of time or maybe they figured they got the job done with the six others. At any rate, it ended the street meetings. I remember going into the prayer room on campus and spending half the night. Finally I decided to just let it all go, settle down and finish my education, get my degree and then go out and do ministry.

Even after all that I got a letter from the school a few weeks later demanding that I "terminate my educational procedures" at the school come spring. They let me stay until spring since we were again pregnant so as not to work undue hardship on us. Only one professor ever came and talked with me personally. He almost persuaded me to settle down and finish my schooling, but I think I had become too hardened from the mistreatment. I continued in my rebellion and stirred up more trouble for the school until they eventually had to threaten me "either get off this campus or we are going to have the police come and throw you off." I left a rather bitter man. Again, I learned that if you take the time to respectfully discuss with young people you have a good chance of turning them from their rebellion. I'm convinced that would have been the case with me.

Out of college and off to Missouri

We moved from the trailer to a house in the country near the church where I was preaching in Missouri. My lessons in human rejection were just beginning. You must understand I was still not saved. It may seem strange to some that a man could be preaching, attending Bible college, holding revival meetings, working in church camps, printing a Christian periodical and still not be saved, but that was indeed the case. I held a two week revival meeting in that church and great things happened. I saw several people accept Jesus as their Savior even though such a thing had not yet happened to me. I had zeal for God, but not according to the knowledge of the truth. Me and the song evangelist had been conducting meetings in the school every day for those two weeks. One day the principal called me up and said he had 5 seniors in his office who wanted to accept Jesus. Although it scared me to death I led them to the Lord. Even a jackass or rooster can bring people to conviction. I saw folks from 8-80 saved in that meeting. We started with one young person the first night (we had a youth gathering just before the main meeting), by the end of the week we had 40 teen-agers coming. It was a great two weeks.

The young lady leading the youth and the singing was working at it night and day. In the middle of the two weeks she came down with a mild heart attack and was confined to bed. I called the elders together and read them James 5:14, 15 "Is anyone among you sick? Let him call for the elders of the church, and let them pray over him, anointing him with oil in the name of the Lord. And the prayer of faith will save the sick, and the Lord will raise him up. And if he has committed sins, he will be forgiven." After reading the passage to the gathered men I asked them "Do you believe this Scripture." One very wise and humble elder said with conviction: "It's in the Bible isn't it?" I replied "well, she has called for you, so let's go." We took oil, anointed and prayed for her and the next night she was back with us and continued to do well all the rest of the next week. It was an anointed revival.

I began preaching in a couple of small country churches in the area as well. Things were looking pretty good. One Sunday night I preached hard against smoking and although in the past almost every guy lit up after church let out, not one did after that message. The next morning I was painting the steps to the church when the chairman of the board showed up to talk to me. He never came to church during the two years time I was there. Often he sat in his front yard in a lawn chair, chewed tobacco and spit in a coffee can beside the chair.

"Bob, I've got to ask you to resign" he said.

"Oh", I stopped painting and looked at him, "Why is that?"

"Because of what you said about tobacco last night."

"All I said was that it's a dirty, unclean habit and Christians ought to be clean."

"We have had smarter and older preachers here than you and none of them ever said anything against it."

About that time he lost a good bit of the tobacco he was chewing and it went streaming down the front of his shirt. Of course I was thinking . . . "Humm . . . that proves my point."

"I'll think about it" was my final reply as he walked away.

I found it intriguing what happened to this elder the next day or two after this confrontation. It was his custom to sit in his front yard in a lawn chair and watch the traffic go by. He had a coffee can handy into which he spit his tobacco juice. He had just got up out of the chair to go into the house when a motorcycle came flying down the highway. The cyclist lost control and came roaring into the yard and literally destroyed the chair he had just vacated. Was it a warning? You be the judge.

The following Wednesday I had a youth meeting in the basement and the board met upstairs. The chairman said "Bob when you are finished downstairs, come up here because we want to talk with you." After the youth meeting I came up and stepped through the door.

Immediately the chairman said. "Bob we have accepted your resignation. This meeting is adjourned."

I was speechless. I was treated unfair at the college and now I was being treated unfair at this church. I didn't expect this from adult Christian leaders. I didn't know they could be so under-handed. I was learning, but it still came as a shock when these Christian adults let me down and treated me so unfair. Bucking church tradition is not an easy course.

BACK TO OAKLAND INTO A CULT

Without any employment or means to make a living we were forced to make a move and we made our way back to Oakland. Here I hooked up with my older brother and we began having Bible studies and prayer meetings in the family. We also held a revival meeting in one of the local churches and another in the Lake Park. We also began printing and publishing "The Enlightener" a small Christian publication that reached a few hundred people. I even did a Christian radio program over a local station for a year. All of this activity and I still wasn't saved, but that was not too much longer in coming, but first I would have to spend a year in rather deep darkness.

What is a cult? There is a certain amount of cultism in most churches, even though one would not define them as a "full-blown" cult. A cult is defined as *a form of idolatry. A system of outward forms, ceremonies, rites and rituals of a group. An extravagant admiration for a person, principle, or group.2* One can see seeds of this in most churches today. It was not so in the first century when the church began under the leadership of the apostles. Many churches have strived to return to the practices and principles of the church of the first century. One such group of churches has defined themselves as "restoration churches" who strive to achieve that goal. None have ever fully achieved it.

In the second and third centuries the churches began to apostatize. The apostle Paul and others saw it coming. He told the elders of Ephesus:

---

2   Webster's New Twentieth Century Dictionary

"For I know this, that after my departure savage wolves will come in among you, not sparing the flock. Also from among yourselves men will rise, speaking perverse things, to draw away the disciples after themselves." Acts 20:29, 30. A careful study of the Scriptures and the early practice of the first century church reveal that they did not have what is common in our churches today: namely the "one-man-pastor-system." When the apostles established churches they did not set themselves or any other one man over those churches. In every case they set a group, a plurality of older and experienced men over those churches. They were called elders, bishops, pastors, shepherds as well as teachers. Always they were a plurality. Never was one man exalted over the others and made to be "chief-pastor." A man named Diotrephes who "loved to have the pre-eminence" III John 9 was one such fellow. He was but a preview of many to come.

It is the weakness of human beings to want someone to rule over them. Israel for example wanted a king like all the other nations. God told Samuel to go ahead and give them one, because they demanded it even though He said "Heed the voice of the people in all that they say to you for they have not rejected you, but they have rejected Me, that I should not reign over them." I Sam. 8:7. It was God's desire to be a personal King and teacher to every individual Israelite, but they would have none of it. They wanted and demanded a man-king. God's people are the same through the centuries. Even under this wonderful new covenant we live by we also often resort to seeking human guidance. God's covenant for us is "For this is the covenant that I will make with the house of Israel after those days, says the Lord: I will put My laws in their mind and write them on their hearts; and I well be their God, and they shall be My people. None of them shall teach his neighbor, and none his brother, saying, 'Know the Lord,' for all shall know Me, from the least of them to the greatest of them." Heb. 8:10, 11. What a precious promise. You don't need prophet, priest, pope, pastor, elder, bishop, etc to "know the Lord". God himself wants to live in you, be yoked to you, to Master you, to dwell in you as a Vine does a branch and lead you in His pathways. But no, we insist on great and powerful men to lead us. We refuse to believe that God can direct our steps (Prov. 3:5, 6). As this spirit developed in the 2nd and 3rd centuries after the apostles the churches lost the inspiration of "the priest-hood of all believers" I Peter 2:9. They quit mutually edifying one another as Paul taught in I Cor. 14 and they began to rely on high-minded and much educated men to lead them. As this apostasy continued it eventually devolved into a supreme teacher/leader in Rome called a pope who ruled the Western churches and a supreme "bishop" in Constantinople who ruled the Eastern churches. Every church had selected from "among themselves" (as Paul had prophesied) one specific person to be the "bishop" of their church. The common people had sacrificed their intimacy with God for the arrogance and self-righteousness of a select "leader." Today he is called a "pastor" or "preacher" or "minister" and often referred to as "Reverend," a term used exclusively for God in the Scriptures. In some churches he is even called "father" a term that Jesus commanded we should never use for our spiritual leaders. (Matt. 23:9).

It was the goal of the Protestant Movement to escape all this corruption and get back to the original structure that Jesus and the apostles had instituted. The apostasy had gone so far and so deep that it would take centuries to recover what had been lost. Not only that, but the powers that had come into being were not about to back down from their domineering and demanding position. Thus a lot of blood was shed by those first reformers, restorers and Protestants. The people in positions of power in our churches today do not resort to shedding blood to maintain their supremacy, but they still are strict, stern and demanding in their aloofness. God's people continue to be in desperate need of a return to the intimacy God has promised under His New Covenant and learn to escape the ongoing influence of "Babylon and her harlots." (Rev. 17:5)

I've said all this about cults and cultism to preface the story of my year in a cult. Perhaps you've heard of Herbert W. Armstrong and his cult of the 60's. I needed to learn that one cannot be saved by his good works, or by belonging to the "right church," or by following certain rules, laws and plans. I had not yet learned of the great and amazing grace of God whereby man is saved. Somehow this man and his teaching intrigued me. It didn't take long to take the bait of "acceptance by performance." I began to follow his demands for certain performances which included dropping out of all other churches, submitting myself to his authority and following his rules. It's rather hard to explain unless you've been there. I was also forbidden to preach unless I was taught and commissioned by him, so I began taking his correspondence course and reading all his books, magazines and literature. You may think it rather ridiculous that a man would follow a false prophet, but be careful. Many pastors today set themselves up over their congregations and present themselves as the man with all the answers . . . or at least the final answer. Unfortunately many folks do become followers of their pastor. That is cultish if not out-right cultism.

SALVATION COMES AT LAST

Toward the end of my year in the cult I was talked into attending a revival meeting in town. My mother convinced me to go. While there a preacher from a nearby church came up to me and asked me to come to his church and hold a revival. He didn't know I was deep in a cult that forbid me to preach. His request sent me deep into a quandary. I wanted so much to preach, but I had to turn him down. I came under deep conviction. I was in agony. I desperately wanted to preach and tell the world about Jesus, but I couldn't. What was I to do? "I know" I thought "I'll go into a season of fervent and continual prayer." Since I couldn't go out and tell the world about Jesus, I could at least pray them in. For two weeks I prayed earnestly and fervently, night and day, almost continually for the whole world. Toward the end of the two weeks I was cutting firewood in my father-in-law's woods. It was winter, toward the end of February, and although it was cold with snow on the ground I found myself frequently stopping the wood cutting in order to kneel in the snow and pray. The conviction had grown to an intense level. I'll never forget the next experience. I knelt at old stump there in the woods and poured my heart out to God with tears streaming down my face. On the one hand I wanted to preach so very much, but on the other hand I felt I would be condemned and disobedient if I did. In that deep inner strain and conflict I finally cried out to the Lord: "You can send me to hell if you want, but I'm gonna go tell the world about Jesus." In my deceived understanding I thought I was literally putting my salvation on the line. I gave up on trying to save myself. I gave up trying to make myself right with God by my works. I rolled it over into His lap as to whether I would go to heaven or hell. It was to be His decision. It was the moment He was waiting for. It was the surrender I needed to make. God thundered all through my being loud and clear. No not in an audible voice, but nevertheless an unmistakable message came through as clear as the cloudless sunny sky above me. "NOW YOU'RE ACCEPTED." Such a joy and peace flooded through my soul. God and I connected. I was warmly embraced. I knew I was in His loving arms. I felt light as a feather. For two weeks I walked around as if I were six feet off the ground. I was born again. I was saved. My sins were gone beneath the blood. I received the Holy Spirit. My name was written in the Lamb's Book of Life. I was henceforth able to echo the words of Paul in II Tim 1:12 "I know whom I have believed and am persuaded that He is able to keep what I have committed to Him until that Day." My salvation was out of my hands and into His. He has never given it back. I'm as saved today as I was that day and every day since and will be from henceforth and forever. Hallelujah.

PART TWO

From salvation to Agape Acres

ETERNAL SECURITY
(ONCE SAVED ALWAYS SAVED)

I did not understand what had happened to me. I still had lots of confusion about many doctrines. You can be right with Jesus and wrong about a lot of other things and still make it to heaven. On the other hand you can be right about everything else under the sun, but if you are wrong about Jesus you are headed for a Christless eternity. It would be a few years before I would understand that this was my day of salvation. It took an old Southern Baptist preacher, a man who became my mentor, to help me understand grace and how it was grace that caught me to glory that eventful day. Although I don't know the exact day it happened, I know it was the last week of February of 1960 and God has not failed or forsaken me one moment since that day.

Believers have allowed this subject to cause controversy, dissension and division among them. It's a subject where we need to learn to agree to disagree. I experienced this long ago. When I was saved, as I've explained earlier in this treatise I knew that my salvation was no longer an effort of mine, but an act of God. I had given over my destiny to His merciful hands. He accepted me because of what Jesus had done for me. It had nothing to do with my performance except to surrender and accept the free gift. My old mentor helped me understand the teaching and doctrine of eternal security. I became comfortable with it; even though the churches I attended believed you can lose your salvation. Most of the time it was not a controversy, but there was one time it became very contentious. I was attending a small Bible study and prayer group in a friend's home. We were having some really good spiritual meetings, but one fellow felt a need to try and correct my beliefs about eternal security. Every week we would go at it and throw Scriptures back and forth in fierce argument, each of us trying to prove our position with plenty of Biblical background. After some time the group got sick of it. They threatened us "Either you two get out of this group, or shut up about the subject, we are tired of hearing your constant wrangling." We agreed to drop the subject and the group continued to get even better as the focus was more and more upon all the good things God has done for us through Jesus Christ. About a year or so later the brother and I were sharing coffee and donuts after the meeting as we rejoiced over all the good that God was doing. It was a great fellowship.

Then he made the statement "God is so good. I don't think I could ever do anything that would cause Him to let go of me."

I stood there rather shocked and finally was able to say "What did you just say?" He stopped short, blinked his eyes, looked down as in deep thought and finally looked up as a smile spread across his face and said "Well, I guess I finally came around didn't I?"

We both laughed, and no, I did NOT say "I told you so." I walked away from that with a new perspective about eternal security. It is not so much a doctrine to teach people or argue about, as an experience that comes from walking close to the Lord. As we draw near to Him, He gives us the "full assurance of faith" that settles our uncertain hearts. I no longer argue the issue. I don't need to. I just need to draw people to Jesus and let Him assure them of His saving, keeping, preserving power found in His great love and grace.

Don't get me wrong, I have plenty of Scriptures to back up the teaching of eternal security, but if a person is convinced he must perform to get assurance he will never grasp it no matter how well I debate the issue. Experience glories over doctrine. When you "know that you know" you don't have to argue or "proof text" your position. God did not call us to preach and teach doctrines so much as He has called us to present Jesus Christ to a hurting, scared, unbelieving world in darkness. We need to live out our joy, love and peace and it will convince folks we have something. Jesus said "By this all will know that you are My disciples, if you have love for one another." John 13:35. When they see Jesus living His life in us then they will be convinced we have something worth seeking. The ultimate dynamic influence we have upon the world is to let them see Jesus walking in our steps. I hope you can see He has been walking "In My Steps" throughout my lifetime. That's the purpose of this book. I want you to see Jesus. See Him alive and well and living in His people today. Our love for one another is one of the best demonstrations of that; love and the full assurance that we are saved kept and secure until His soon coming return.

THE MOVE NORTH AND INTO BUSINESS WITH MY BROTHERS

I did throw off the shackles of the cult shortly after being saved. I took all that literature to a junk pile and threw it as far as I could. It wasn't easy. The tentacles of that false prophet and his false teaching were clawed deep in my spirit. It felt like pulling thorns out of my brain as I dragged the stuff out of my car and flung it away, but I drove away from that junk pile a free man. Hallelujah. I even tore the pages out of my diary for that year and threw them away. I sort of regretted that later, since I've kept a detailed journal of my life since I was 16. That year is missing from the journal.

We moved 40 miles north to a small town South of Champaign-Urbana and began a 10 year period of building a construction company along with my four brothers, a friend, a cousin and others we hired along the way. We started attending a church that came as close as any I've ever attended to doing their meetings according to the pattern laid out in I Cor. 14 by Paul. We didn't follow the pattern of most churches which are still trapped in the "one-man-pastor-system." During Sunday meetings different men in the church would take turns bringing edifying messages. Sometimes several would share the pulpit on Sunday mornings. All this was overseen by a plurality of elders also known as pastors/bishops/shepherds (All words describing the same office in the Scriptures). Those were good and edifying times. One Sunday a brother got up and preached the whole book of James from memory. It was indeed edifying. It was here I preached my first message on the great and amazing grace of God.

Of all the strange places I took my text from Song of Solomon 1:2 "Let Him kiss me with the kisses of His mouth; for your love is better than wine." I expounded on His great, compassionate and intimate love for us sinners. As we respond to that over-whelming love we become as intoxicated on it as much or more than what folks are on wine. It is meant that we "lose our lives" in that seducing love and grace. It was a very anointed message and my old mentor was there with his shouts of "amen" to keep me fired up and going.

He and I began going about helping other churches get started. Eventually we settled into a church in the North end of Urbana where we found freedom to edify the saints, pray with abandon and receive encouragement to go out and evangelize. We had many Bible studies and prayer meeting across the twin cities.

STREET MINISTRY AND OTHER GOOD WORKS

I had a growing conviction to do ministry on the U. of I. campus. One Sunday night I went around and asked each man in the church service to go with me to pass out tracts. Not a one felt led to go and turned me down. I didn't feel the courage to start doing it alone. I needed at least one person. Not a one volunteered. After I left the church I drove toward the campus. I prayed: "God I'm gonna drive by the campus. If you give me the courage between here and there I'll stop and start passing out tracts. If you don't, I'm just gonna keep on driving home." I pulled up and stopped at a stop light in down-town Urbana. A horn honked behind me and a fellow came running out of the car and jumped in the seat beside me. "God would not let me rest until I consented to go with you" he said. It was the first of many trips to the campus and God always provided a partner to go with me.

We saw lots of signs, wonders and miracles during that ministry. We passed out 1000's of tracts. We talked to many folks about their relationship with Jesus Christ. One night I was standing on a street corner passing out tracts when the Lord spoke to my heart and said "Take one step to the left." As I did a water balloon splatted where I had been standing. I didn't give the perpetrators the pleasure of even looking up. I just casually strolled on down the street smiling to myself saying "thank you Lord." Another time I saw a fellow coming toward us and heard the Lord distinctly say "Give that fellow a tract." He turned toward his parked car a half block away from us. I knew he was to receive a tract and I told the brother with me "that guy's car will not start until we get to him." We could hear the car grinding away trying to start. When we got next to it I motioned for him to roll down the window. As he did I handed him a tract and said "Sir, if you'll take this tract home and read it your car will start." He looked at me kinda funny and took it, then reached down and tried to start his car and it instantly started. I betcha he read that tract. You never know how far a tract will minister.

Me and my mentor started going down-town Champaign on Sunday mornings. We prayed with folks at the train and bus stations. We passed out tracts to Sunday morning "walkers" and runners. We often passed by the XXX theatre and stuck a tract or two under the ticket window. One Sunday morning the cleaning lady stepped out of the theatre and asked "Are you the guys that keep sticking the tracts under the ticket window?" We rather sheepishly said "Yes, maam." She said "I would like more of them. I sent some to my son in California and he got saved by reading them." How amazing and what a great sense of humor God has to even use a XXX rated theatre to save a lost soul. Another time me and a partner were walking down a dark street that was empty of people, but I heard the Lord say "Pass out a tract." I thought it strange that He asked me pass out a tract when there was no one in sight. I asked my partner "Do you want a tract? The Lord is telling me to pass out a tract." He pointed to the back of a nearby parking lot where he had spied some kids making out in a parked car back in the darkness. I would not have interrupted their "love scene" without that gentle nudge from God. I boldly walked up to their car, tapped on the window and broke things up. They rolled down the window, looking at me a bit angry. I handed them several tracts and said "Here, God wants you to have these." I then turned and started back across the parking lot to my waiting partner. About half way across the lot the kids came barreling out of the car and caught up with me saying

"What are you doing out here making fun of religion?" They took that attitude from the title of the tract: "Religion is for the birds."

I asked: "Did you read that tract?"

"Well no" they said.

"It's short; take a minute to read it." I waited silently as they all began reading. The tract was one we had written. It told how Christianity is a relationship more than a religion. It also told how when Jesus returns we shall be caught up with Him in the air like so many birds. After they read it they said "Oh," and quietly returned to their car. During a home-coming week-end several of us passed out 5000 tracts on the crowded streets and campus. We found very few laying in the gutters. One wonders where all those tracts traveled and what came from them. God has promised "So shall My word be that goes forth from My mouth; It shall not return to Me void, But it shall accomplish what I please, and it shall prosper in the thing for which I sent it." Isa. 55:11. God's word is truth and the truth sets people free and saves their souls. All those tracts were laced with the word of God. Only eternity will tell what fruit came from that ministry of several years.

During those years in the C-U area we saw several miracles and wonders. I was in many prayer meetings with my mentor and his mother Grandma Blue. She was a real prayer warrior and I can remember her storming heaven many times in behalf of her other son Monty. Almost every time we had a prayer meeting she would pray for Monty. I can still hear her today praying "God whatever it takes bring Monty to his knees." A couple of years after Grandma Blue died my mentor Doc Blue got a phone call from Monty's family in Chicago. Monty had been in a terrible car accident. They left part of his brains in the car and at the hospital they didn't do much for him because they didn't expect him to live through the night. Doc and I continued to pray for him. He did live through the night so they thought they probably ought to do some patch work on him. They still didn't expect him to live very long, but even if he did he would be nothing but a vegetable lying on a bed, and he would never regain consciousness. They believed too much of his brain had been left in the car seat. After a week or so he began to come conscious, but he was not coherent. The medical staff said this was worse because he would never become rational. Let me make a long story short. Over the weeks and months that followed he continued to have longer and longer times of being conscious and also longer periods of being rational. Eventual he was completely healed and back to normal; with one exception. He went into that car wreck a lost and drunken soul, but as he came out of the injuries he was a saved soul praising the Lord. Grandma Blue's prayers were answered. Don't ever stop praying for your family members. God may have to knock some of their brains out to get their attention.

Another interesting miracle came out of prayer meetings we were having in a church in the North end of Urbana. A brother's car was having bad transmission problems. When he went to work of a morning he would slide a pan under the transmission and catch the fluid that drained out and then dump it back into the transmission. When he went home at night he would again put the pan back under and in the morning pour the fluid back in the transmission. This had been going on for days. He asked us to pray about getting a newer car, but his finances were tight. We prayed that God would step in and help the guy out. The next morning he slid the pan out and it was dry. He checked the fluid and it was up and full. He drove to work and put the pan under again. When he got off work the pan was dry and the transmission checked full. It was the first time I ever heard of God healing a transmission on a car.

GREAT DIFFICULTIES IN BUSINESS

We experienced God's hand in directing circumstances when we bought a car and when we bought a house. Again and again He stepped into our situations and showed His merciful miracle working hand. We saw this vividly when our growing company almost went bankrupt. We had bid our first five houses to build. Up to then we had built farm buildings, garages, room additions and done remodel jobs. We got the bids on the five houses. When we closed on the first one we discovered we had not made a dime of profit and barely covered the material expenses. We had four more to go. We tightened our belts, mortgaged our homes, started working 6 days a week and prayed for God's help. It was looking really bad, but only one creditor turned us over to a credit agency. We were really struggling and it looked like we were going to go under. During that time we had been doing jobs on the U. of I. farms. If you wanted them to keep sending you bid proposals you had to keep turning in estimates. If you came upon a job you didn't want, you just bid it unreasonably high so that you would not get the job, but still get more proposals. A bid proposal came along that was busting out concrete in hog confinement sheds and digging out and pouring circulating troughs for a different kind of hog confinement. We had decided we didn't want that stinky, hard work so we bid it very high. Everyone else must have done the same thing, because we got the job. It was a sizable job and was a big factor in getting us through the slump. It proved to be a very dirty, stinky, hard job, but it paid off big and saved our necks. There were times I lifted old tiles out of the ditches as hog manure dripped off both of my elbows. I felt like the prodigal who "would fain have filled his belly with the husks that the swine did eat." It was quite humiliating but God was good. After a few years of this struggle we looked back and realized we had never missed paying our men and ourselves wages every week of those tough times. God made it work.

LEADINGS TO MINISTRY
IN VILLA GROVE

I got in a small group that was on fire with seeking God and prayer. I had quit work with the idea of going full time in ministry. I just knew God would open doors and I would get a church or find some kind of ministry that would meet our expenses. Well, in spite of all the prayer and earnest search I was about to starve my family and getting deep in debt. I finally had to return to work. As I sought the Lord with this small group the Lord let me know that I was worshiping the ministry instead of Him. As I changed my attitude and repented the Lord opened doors for me to preach. I ended up pastoring a church in Villa Grove for a couple of years. The Lord was strong on me there and lots of souls were being saved and lives being changed. My mentor came down and helped me put on a two-week revival. I preached and he conducted the singing and directed a choir. The Lord's hand was so heavy on me I could hardly breathe before I was to preach. I tried sitting in the audience or in the choir and nothing helped. Finally I went in a room in back of the pulpit and lay on my face before the Lord until it was time for me to preach and they would come in and tell me. Once I stood in the pulpit I was fine and the Lord poured out His Spirit. With all this success I was hearing the Lord say over and over: "Bob, this is just a beginning, this is just a beginning." Things were about to open for us to move to Oakland and begin a ministry on 15 acres that would eventually be called "Agape Acres."

One night when I was preaching a little 3 year old girl asked her mother who that man was standing next to pastor Bob. Mom didn't see anyone and asked the little daughter what the man looked like. The girl said "he is all dressed in white." She asked her if she had ever seen the man in white before. She said "yes mommy, when you are up there singing he stands beside you."

A GREAT TIME WITH DAD IN COLORADO

Another interesting incident took place shortly before we made the move to Oakland. Our dad had been making a yearly trip to Colorado to hunt deer and elk. He had been going for 15 years and I realized that none of us five boys had ever gone with him. I decided to go and asked him if that would be okay. He was excited to have me join him and the group of 20 or so who often went with him. Knowing that I was not accustomed to climbing mountains I began a rigorous routine of exercises to prepare me for the challenge. We spent 10 days in an old cabin 10,000 feet up in the mountains. There was an unusual amount of snow that fall. We had to wade snow 3 and 4 feet deep. That first day I was breaking trail for my ageing dad. (He was 73 and I was 33). After awhile he noticed I was huffing and puffing and he said "Son, let me break trail for awhile." I could barely keep up with the tough old bird. All the rest of the party went to town every night and left me and dad up at the cabin. After a couple of days I asked him

"Wouldn't you rather go down and party with the boys instead of staying up here in the mountain?"

"Oh" he said "I don't want to leave you alone up here by yourself."

"Dad" I said "I'm 33 years old, I'll be fine, and I like my solitary times anyhow." "Well" he said, "if you're sure you'll be okay." Although dad never spoke the words "I love you" I knew by the way he treated me those 10 days that he proved that fatherly love was in his heart.

Like I said, dad had been going out there for 15 years and although he always brought back a deer or two and even a bear once, he had never bagged an elk. One of the days we were out I had a big bull elk come right in my direction. I knew by the direction he was headed he would pass by me and go right toward dad. I had to make a quick decision. Shall I shoot him or let dad finally get an elk. It was an easy decision and as the elk passed by me I yelled "Dad, you've got an elk coming right at you." I heard the loud boom and knew he had bagged his prey. I felt real good in giving him the chance to get his first elk. Later he brought the liver in and said

"Here son, cook this up for supper."

I responded "I'll cook it, but you are going to be the one to eat it." I love liver gravy but can't stand the taste of liver. As he sat there smacking his lips and chuffing down the liver he kept saying "Oh son, you really should try this. It's so good." I finally relented and took a piece just to keep him quiet. I ended up eating as much of it as he did. I've never eaten liver since, but there was something about being 10,000 feet up in the mountains, fresh liver from an elk, and just being in great fellowship with my dad that made that liver turn out delicious. I treasure those memories of being with dad those 10 days as some of my better memories.

It was dad's last trip west. Perhaps he had been waiting for one of us boys to join him. I'm so glad I did. Sadly our youngest brother was killed in a car accident shortly after we got home. I was thankful it didn't happen while we were in Colorado. I would not have wanted to make that drive home with that sorrow in the car. Davey had been telling us for a few years that he would never live to see 30 (he was 24) and that he would never get married. His fiancée was killed along with him just a couple of weeks before they were to be married. I think losing her baby son caused mom's heart to be all the more opened up to be mom and grandma to all the young people that were going to be coming to Agape Acres. That move was coming within the next year.

PART THREE

*The seven years of Agape Acres
and 50 Holy Happenings*

THE PURCHASE AND BEGINNINGS OF AGAPE ACRES

Agape Acres is 15 acres of woods, a small creek, foot trails through the woods, two houses, an old barn and a wealth of memories. Forty years ago it was a haven for the Jesus People or Christ Kids as they were called in the East Central Illinois area. Dozens and scores came from all over the area to celebrate the work of Jesus Christ in the lives of people today. The last Saturday of the month became a regular time for what we called "Holy Happenings", a 9:00 a.m to a 9:00 p.m. experience of food, fun, fellowship and ministry all over the property, but especially in seven points of inspiration: our home, the great commission cross, the pavilion, the barn, the prayer cells, the baptistery and Andrew's cross. Hundreds of kids (and adults) were saved, filled with the Spirit, baptized, and went out everywhere to spread the faith and love they had discovered in Jesus Christ. Eventually 50 Holy Happenings were experienced over a 7 year period during the early and mid-seventies.

When and how did it begin? We were living in Tolono in the 60's as God began to put the pieces together for this coming ministry. My wife's dad lived just down the road from this piece of property. He was alone, having lost his wife just a few years before. Peggy wanted to live close to him during his latter years so she could help take care of him in his fading health. Although I was in sympathy with her, I did not want to return to my home town. I was willing to go to Russia, China, Africa, or anywhere besides my home town. "A prophet is not without honor except in his home town" was warning enough to make me highly reluctant to return. We had noticed these 15 acres of woods with a small cottage and thought it would be ideal in that it was close to her dad, but we had heard that many tried to buy it for years and the owner was not the least bit interested in selling it.

On a Memorial Day 1969 Peggy crossed paths with this owner in the cemetery and she told him: "If you ever want to sell that property we would like to have a chance at buying it." He looked at her very surprised and said "That's strange, for the first time in my life the thought came to me this morning that I should sell the property." (Is that God's timing or what?) Then he asked "What do want to do with it?" She said; "Well, we want to live close to my dad, and we would like to make it into a gathering place for Christians; some sort of campground."

"Well," he said, "that's interesting. I had made up my mind that if I did sell it, I would not sell it to some farmer who would cut down the woods and plow it up for planting. It has been used through the years for people and I want to see it continue to be used for people." (It was a gathering place on the 4th of July around the turn of the century for a few years.) By December 7th of that year, Peggy's birthday, we signed the papers to purchase the property and spent the next year preparing it for our move from a 7 room house into a 3 room house with no kitchen or bathroom.

I was still reluctant to move, but God began impressing on me that He wanted to use us and the property for ministry. He assured me that if I would follow His leading I would see the Gospel go to all those places I wanted to go. The gospel would go to the whole world from this tiny 15 acres. I was certain that was going to happen before we ever moved onto the property. I was preaching in a small Baptist church in Villa Grove during that year and God was pouring out His Spirit and whispering in my spirit "Bob, this is just a beginning." We made the trip here every week-end and proceeded to turn the little 3 room house into what would eventually become a 15 room house with two baths, a garage, shop and separate apartment over the garage. Every time I walked on the property I was drawn to intense and prevailing prayer. The theme of my prayer was "God, do it again today. Do what you did in the first century. Don't let yourself be known as a God of antiquity, but a God at hand today." Again and again, He assured me the Gospel would go into the entire world from this property. The prayers developed into prophecy and I was fully assured great times were coming.

Although we had built a basement under a sizable addition and had that addition closed in, we were a long ways from having anything finished when we moved August 1st of 1970. We moved out of the 7 room house into 3 rooms. Furniture and boxes were stacked to the ceiling. Our oldest moved in with grandpa down the road and the two girls we managed to fit into bunk beds. Peggy had a bed on the couch and I made a pallet on the floor that first night. As I lay back from the day's work to sleep, I broke out in laughter. When Peggy inquired what was wrong with me I replied: "For the first time in my life I know that I'm exactly where God wants me."

We began attending a small church just outside of Oakland. God immediately connected my heart to several teen-agers there and they became joined to me. We were equally convinced that the love of God and faith in Jesus was the great need of our generation. After a lengthy time of prayer and praise at the altar together we were convinced God was doing something in our area. One night during a revival meeting in that church I was driven by the Spirit to the altar where I cried before the Lord like I've never done before or since. The Spirit was breaking down all my resistance and preparing me to move in His power and love. I soaked and stained that old altar bench with my tears and I was pleased years later when a brother testified one day in a church I was attending that he had been asked to refinish the altar. He refused and said those stains were standing evidence of how God had worked in the lives of many people and he would not be a part of removing them.

I became a youth leader in that little church and the kids began to come out to the property to help me pour concrete and build on our house. They liked the property and a desire for meetings here began to grow in all of us. There were many games of ping pong in our basement and times of Bible study and prayer. The kids loved to play guitars and sing and we began to have opportunities to go out to churches and share the joy and love that was growing in our hearts. As more and more kids took more interest I saw the need of someone stepping forward to lead these kids. I prayed God to raise someone up and more and more the attention was pointed to me.

About this time I heard of a seminar being held by Campus Crusade in a nearby city. The seminar was on "How to start and carry on a ministry to youth in your community." I took one of the teen-agers with me and we went to the seminar. On the hour drive there I kept thinking and sharing with John: "We don't need this seminar. We don't need Campus Crusade. All we need is Jesus and just trust Him to put it together." When we got there the first thing the leader said when he stood before us was: "You don't need me. You don't need this seminar. You don't need Campus Crusade. All you need is Jesus." (Another very "God moment" huh?)

We returned and began to have meetings in the high school. 60 to 70 kids showed up. The Jesus Movement across the nation was in full swing. One night a group of local preachers and leaders showed up and wanted to know what was going on. They feared we might teach doctrines to their young people contrary to their church's beliefs. I said "I'm just sharing Jesus with them. I want them to love and trust Him and the rest will fall into place. It's your job to teach them your church's particular doctrines." Although most of them saw no problem with our work, some were a bit apprehensive and withdrew their kids from the group. However, the group continued to prosper. The kids were sharing their faith on the streets and in the school. One youngster told how he accepted Jesus sitting on the bathroom stool as the kid on the next stool witnessed to him.

INVOLVEMENT WITH THE FBI

Some folks were scared that we were some sort of cult or subversive group, perhaps even communists. One lady even called the FBI and convinced them to investigate us. After their secret investigation they reported back to her that this country needs more people doing what Bob Clapp is doing to help young people get their lives together. I guessed we passed their approval with flying colors. I never knew anything about all this until a few years later. One day I got a phone call and the fellow on the other end of the line told me he was from the FBI. I figured it was one of my friends pulling a joke, but I played along with him. "Do you know Bud Frisco?" he asked. (Not his real name). "Yeah, I know him why?" They were getting my curiosity up now. "Well, we have had something develop with him where we could use your help." "Okay" I said "if you are really from the FBI how is it you know my name and how do you get the idea I can help you?" He then told me the story of my frightened neighbor and their thorough investigation. I was finally convinced he was legit. "All right, how can I help you?" They told me that Bud had called them to do something about a cult in a nearby town. Bud's son was joined to that group and the leaders had insisted that they were not to let the grand-parents visit and have any effect on their kids. Bud, needless to say, was furious and demanded the FBI do something about the group. They tried to convince him it was a religious matter and beyond their jurisdiction. He got all the more angry and screamed at them "If you're not going to do something, by God, I will and I'm gonna do it tonight." The agent begged me to go have a talk with the guy and try to cool him down. I agreed to.

I walked into Bud's shop and began a visit. When I asked him how things were going he stopped his work and said "Not so good." He explained the situation to me. I said "Bud, when I was younger and starting out on this Christian walk I was also sort of like that." I explained how when we are given time and space we grow out of such radicalism. "Give your son some time. I'm sure he will come out of that attitude. He knows you love your grandkids and want to be with them. He will mellow in time." I probably sounded more sure of myself than what I was. As we talked I could see he was settling down and doing some deep thinking. I still didn't know if I had given him enough to change his mind about doing something tragic. Finally when I was starting to leave he said. "It's a good thing you came by and had this talk with me." "Why is that?" I asked. "I was gonna do something tonight that I probably would have regretted." I do believe the Spirit of God moved upon him to leave the shot-gun in the closet and give God time to resolve matters over time. I left with a sigh of relief. Sure enough it was no time before he was allowed to have his grand-kids back in his life. God works in strange ways His wonders to perform.

I was having a hard time forgiving the sister who had called the FBI on me. I did what I knew I had to do to get past it. I went to my basement, got on my face on that concrete floor and prayed for the power to forgive and let it go. The longer I prayed the more I felt the pendulum swing away from the anger and unforgiveness. I started to get up as the bad attitude went away and I knew I had forgiven her. The big hand of God pressed down upon me and He spoke deep in my heart "You aren't through yet." I returned to prayer. As I prayed I felt the "pendulum" swing even further to the right and I knew I not only had forgiven her, but I was praying rich and bountiful blessings down upon her. God's agape love for her flooded my soul and I got up shouting "hallelujah." I felt so good about her I decided to go to a youth revival she was holding and took a seat way in the back. I was thrilled to see how God poured out His love, joy and peace on that gathering as she led it. God is so good isn't He?

We took a couple of car-loads of kids to a neighboring town where the Jesus Movement seemed to be in full swing. Zeal for Jesus and His way was growing. We took a couple of car-loads to northern Indiana where several groups of Jesus People were gathering for a couple of days of celebration. We all came back fired up and shouting the praises of a wonderful Savior, Friend and King. We were all getting "turned on" to Jesus.

THE FIRST HOLY HAPPENINGS

Our first "Holy Happening" on the property developed from this fervor. It "happened" on July 31, 1971 and went from 9:00 on a Saturday morning to 9:00 Saturday night. We had put together a 40' tall cross, decked it with lights and stood it up in our front yard. 150 kids showed for that first happening. We stood the cross up at the start and made a circle around it in prayer and praise. (A teen-ager who was later saved and joined us happened to drive by and saw the circle of prayer. He passed by later that night when we had again gathered for a prayer circle and he thought we had been praying in that circle all day.) We baptized 8 young people in the Oakland Lake in the afternoon of that first "Happening."

We had study groups all over the property that day and had at least a couple of meetings in the barn. We filed the group through our kitchen and served them a meal. (Later we would build a pavilion with a kitchen, bathrooms and sizable dining and meeting area.)

The seven points of inspiration would come into play each in their own time. If there was any doubt in my mind about the gospel going into all the world, it was removed as I walked back to the barn during that first happening. I came upon four young people in the middle of the property holding hands in prayer. Three were exchange students and one was from America. One was from France, one from Africa, and one from Yugoslavia. God "spoke" loud and clear to my spirit: "I told you the gospel would go into all the world from this property." The girl from France led 5 people to the Lord on her trip back home. She has carried on ministry over the years with Wycliffe Bible translators. She had accepted Jesus in my brother's home earlier. Although she had gone back to the house where she was living and wrote me a letter saying "I don't believe this is real. I feel nothing different," she tore up the letter the next morning and has walked in the joy of the Lord since.

A great ministry had begun on Agape Acres and the surrounding area. People would come from all over Illinois, Indiana and Missouri. Some came from foreign countries like the exchange students. The effects of what God would do on Agape Acres would be felt around the globe. Our kids joined 100,000 other "Jesus People" at Explo 72 in Dallas, Texas for an explosion of faith, love, joy and praise. Christian coffee houses sprang up in a number of cities around us and many nights were spent there in Bible studies, prayer meetings and great fellowship. Many churches opened their doors to the ministry these kids brought. It was indeed an old-fashioned revival that swept across the nation and around the world. I question whether the Jesus Movement of the 70's was ever given the recognition by the organized church that it deserved. Unlike many revivals before, this one was chiefly centered on teen-agers and perhaps that kept it from having the recognition it deserved.

THE NAME AGAPE ACRES

We are often asked "Where did you get the name 'Agape Acres?'" "Agape" is a Greek word for "love." There are three primary words for love in the Greek language (the New Testament was originally written in Greek). The three are agape, phileo and eros. Eros is the root word from which we get "erotic." Yes, it is a word that describes sensual or sexual love. It is the attraction between the two sexes. That can be good or bad. Without it, we probably wouldn't be here. Most intimate relationships begin with this kind of love. It might be called that "love at first sight" kind of love. You see the shapely body, the pretty or handsome face, the beautiful flowing hair, the smile, the twinkle in the eye (or the wink), and you are tuned in and turned on. It can be a good start, but if something deeper doesn't come along it's not going to last. Hair turns grey and falls out. Body shapes can take drastic changes. A charming attitude at a party can become coercive in the early morning hours of the next day. With 50% of marriages today ending up in the divorce courts it's easy to believe that most of them never got beyond the eros level of love.

The second Greek word to be looked at is phileo. We get our word "friend" from phileo. Friends have learned to be good and kind to one another. They have discovered that love can be "exchanged." If you do someone good, they will often do you good back. That tends to work well. When a couple go out of their way to do nice things to one another an "exchanged love" develops. That works well as long as both parties keep it up. It's sort of a 50/50 relationship. As long as the give and take continues it works. Many marriages last a life-time with such a love. It works until one or the other quits giving back. We don't like to just give and give and never get anything in return. When that happens the relationship is in big trouble and if the next level isn't reached pretty quickly it's going to be another trip to the divorce court.

The third Greek word is agape. This is the 100% unconditional love. This love says "No matter how you treat me, I'm going to love you." It's the kind of love that God has. It's the kind of love that took Jesus to the cross and caused Him to look down on his persecutors and say "Father forgive them, they know not what they do." It's the kind of love that keeps on giving and giving even when there is no response or sign of appreciation. It is completely unselfish. It's the love described in I Cor. 13 "Love never gives up. Love cares more for others than for self. Love doesn't want what it doesn't have. Loves doesn't strut, doesn't have a swelled head, doesn't force itself on others, isn't always 'me first,' doesn't fly off the handle, doesn't keep score of the sins of others, doesn't revel when others grovel, takes pleasure in the flowering of truth, puts up with anything, trusts God always, always looks for the best, never looks back, but keeps going to the end. Love never dies."[3] I don't think one can ever achieve this level of love without Jesus being given first place in your heart. It is virtually Jesus living His life in you, which He is more than willing to do if we will just allow Him that freedom. And that is where we came up with the title of "Agape Acres." It's our goal more than our achievement, and we trust God to help us grow for a life-time in that direction.

---

[3]   From *The Message* by Eugene H. Peterson

Miracles Wonders and Signs

I don't know why God chose me and my family to be a part of this great movement. I'm thankful He did. I never felt worthy of the blessings He poured out, but I cannot deny the miracles, wonders, and blessings that came. I have not embellished these stories of that exciting time. They speak for themselves. I don't understand all that happened, I just tell you like it was and you can draw your own conclusions. It was a work of God. It wasn't the product of any church or religious organization. God led us to do and experience what we did as individuals and groups that hungered to see Him do again today what He has done in the past. And He did. These are only a few of the stories. I saw what I saw and experienced what I experienced, but many things happened around me, all over this property that I was never an eye-witness to.

I have put out "feelers" to some who were here during those years. I asked them to share with me some of their memories and experiences. Here is an example of something I had no part of and did not witness. Stan, my oldest brother was very active here during those years. At a recent reunion of our family I told him I was writing this story. I asked him to share some of the experiences he had of those years. He told how he and another brother had been asked to pray for a woman who had a paralyzed hand. She could not open her hand and had not been able to for years. When he and the other brother approached her Stan commanded her "Open your hand." She replied "Stan, you know I can't do that." Again he looked her in the eye and said with a little more emphasis "Open your hand." When he commanded her the third time she obeyed and shouted for joy as her hand was made whole. That is one of many experiences that took place on this property during those years of which I had no first-hand experience.

You see, it was not about me, or my brother, or any special group, church or organization. It was from the beginning a work of God. In spite of our weaknesses, fears, doubts, questions, and short-comings God came and did a work. He led folks here and anointed the work to minister to them. One group came from a town about 40 minutes away and a cloud in the shape of a cross led them all the way. (I did see that cross as it continued to move on past the property). It's been over 40 years and I probably should have written all this years ago. I have no doubt forgotten many things, but some I can never forget. I do remember enough to convince anyone with an open mind that God still does miracles today. He still leads people to trust in Him. He still shares and instills His love and grace into common folks. What He did here, He does anywhere and everywhere that people realize "Jesus is the Answer."

Another experience came at the beginning; in fact it was our first of what would eventually be 50 Holy Happenings. It was a march we made from the Lake Park in Oakland across town to the down-town park. We had 20-30 kids carrying a banner that stretched across the street which read "JESUS IS THE ANSWER." People lined the streets and gathered around the down-town square to watch this spectacle (marches were taking place all across the nation at that time and many developed into riots . . . ours was peaceful.) When we got to the square we gathered in a circle and sang some songs of praise. There was a stump there and God impressed me to get up on it and preach the gospel. I didn't. I regret to this day that I was disobedient. Yes, we failed at times. We were far from perfect, but God nonetheless poured out many blessings, miracles and wonders. He still does.

There was another experience I had in that first year of intense prayer and prophecy. On one of those prayerful times I was sitting at an old picnic table under the oak trees on the North side of the property. I was impressed to open my Bible and turned to Lamentations. Chapter two verse nineteen burned into my heart and my prayers: "Arise, cry out in the night: in the beginnings of the watches pour out thine heart like water before the face of the Lord: lift up thy hands toward Him for the life of thy young children, that faint for hunger in the top of every street." (KJV) I wept over that Scripture as it blossomed in my hungry heart. I did indeed yearn for the lives of many children who were indeed fainting for hunger on the streets of America. Drugs, alcohol and promiscuity were wide spread "in the top of every street." I touched my tears with my finger and anointed the verse in my old KJV Bible. It still carries the stain of those tears some 40 years later. It was an impacting time and I knew God was going to use me, my family and this property to rescue and minister to many young people. The stage and my heart were being set for just such a ministry.

Another incident comes to mind during those months of preparation before any of the teen-agers began to come. I had dug a basement on the South side of the 3 barren rooms of the little cottage. I had laid the foundation and had concrete blocks laid about half way up. I slept alone in the little cottage that night. A storm came and raged. I heard the walls collapse like thunder due to the very heavy downpour of rain. I screamed and cursed at God "What are you trying to do to me?" Then I fell to my knees and humbly asked for the power to praise Him even in this trying storm of events. He whispered gently to my heart: "Bob, I'm just trying to put grit into you so that you will stay with something even when the going gets tough." Twice more those walls came down before I finally gave up the idea of putting in the basement. I ordered out a bull-dozer and came down on the week-end with the full intention of burying the attempt to build a basement. Unfortunately, the owner of the dozer was just pulling out with the dozer on a low-boy as I pulled in. "I've got to have this on a job . . . sorry" was his reply. I stood dejected on the bank beside the flooded hole where I had already thrown in a bunch of junk to bury with the failed basement. I thought "I can't build it and I can't fill it up, I can do neither."

I was aware that my brother Stan had walked up beside me on my right and my father-in-law on my left. I don't remember to this day the exact words they spoke, but they both agreed and encouraged me to believe I could still build that basement. Faith was reborn and I have set on the bottom step of that basement several times since and marveled how God "put the grit into me" to see it finished. It has served well, not only for plumbing, heating and storage, but many young people came and played ping pong, had Bible studies and prayer meeting and at one time we even printed and published a Christian newspaper there. A lesson of endurance was learned in that trial that took me through many difficult times in days and years to come.

THE TRANSFORMED OLD BARN

So much happened in the old barn. It was originally built for use as an old rendering plant. The place was called "The Stink Plant." Farmers who had animals die in the pasture or from some unknown reason that rendered the meat and carcass useless would bring the animals here to be processed. The critters were dragged onto a concrete platform and butchered. The fluids were drained off to a couple of holding cells down over the hill where they were held until a good flooding rain came and were then released to flow down the creek. (Those holding cells became our present day "prayer cells.) The animals were skinned and the hides were stored in the "hide room" to be sold. The carcass was then moved to a boiling or steam tank on the opposite side of the barn where it was cooked down so the bones could be separated from the meat. The meat was fed to hogs and the bones were ground up in a near-by building for some use. Thousands of animals were thus rendered during the 20's and 30's. Some of the equipment from those days is still in evidence including a very tall chimney where the smoke from the cooking ascended.

When we purchased the property the barn was being used for storing hay. When the kids began to come and hold meetings we made bleachers out of the hay for them to sit in a half circle. At one gathering early on, they painted messages all over the barn and a cross on the roof. "Jesus is Coming," "God loves you," and many such slogans were painted and most remain to this day. A couple of crosses hang from the roof inside. One old rugged one hangs in the center of the barn. It came from the Christian coffee house in Charleston that was called "The Fishnet." It was one of several coffee houses in the area that developed during the Jesus Movement and saw the salvation of many young people. The other cross is made of white painted boards and it came from a VBS in a local church. There are writings around the inside of the barn as well as on the outside. Much later, after the hay was removed we poured a concrete floor and in it are many messages such as "only one life will soon be past, only what's done for Christ will last."

We had a rope tied to the roof for a swing and during one of those first meetings the kids would swing from the "bleachers" to the concrete platform and from there give their testimony before swinging back to join the crowd. They brought guitars and drums and played their joy and zeal in old and new Christian music. It was very informal and spontaneous.

The loose hay down in the middle was probably about two feet deep. At one meeting one of the kids lost a contact lens in that hay. "No problem" one of them shouted, "Let's just praise the Lord and hunt for it." They did, and they almost immediately found it.

Once a year, generally the last week-end of July we had a 3 day Holy Happening. Kids and adults came and camped in the woods or slept in the barn and the pavilion. After one of those camps I came to the barn on Monday morning to do some clean up. Bumble bees would hardly let me in the barn. "Where in the world did all these bees come from?" I thought. I rounded up some sprays and gas and proceeded to do battle with them until I had wiped them out. The battle led to a nest in the center of the hay bleachers where I found a huge nest. God had subdued those bees all week-end. We had climbed all over that hay and no doubt stepped again and again on that huge nest, yet not a single bee was seen. God turned them loose on Monday morning and it took me awhile to conquer and control them.

We had 50 Holy Happenings here and most of them centered on the barn for our meetings. When the weather was inclimate we had meetings in the pavilion, but that came later on. We also built wood bleachers after the hay was hauled away. A barn across the road was torn down and we salvaged a lot of wood from that to build the present bleachers.

I'm sitting in the barn while writing this and it's raining a real downpour. It reminds me of the time we had such a down-pour during one of our meetings. I was trying to teach and the noise of rain on the tin roof was so loud I could shout at the top of my lungs and not be heard. We all turned to our Bibles to quietly read while waiting for the rain and noise to let up. God gave me Jeremiah 10:13 "When He utters His voice, there is a multitude of waters in the heavens." I passed the Scripture around for all to read.

A couple of teens from Chicago came by for one of those 3-day camp-outs. They thought we were having Rock Concerts here. I told them "Yes, we have "solid rock" concerts." They were about ready to leave but I implored them to stay and see what this is all about. They stayed. By Sunday night things had changed in their lives. They got up and shared before the group: "We came down here to get high on these" one said as he took off his hat and revealed several reefers, "but you people have shown us something a whole lot better and we want what you have." They both got saved and baptized and returned to Chicago. They were members of a gang and one of them was held in a basement and his gang members threatened to kill him if he did not renounce Jesus. He told them "If you kill me I'll just go home to be with Jesus, but I'm not turning my back on Him." They let him go. One of the boys became a preacher and is a pastor to this day.

(Wow, is the present storm getting bad. Makes me think the devil doesn't want this to be printed and published. I'm even having difficultly finding a dry place in the old leaky barn to do my typing. Maybe he hates the next story I'm about to write.)

Battling Satan and Demons

During one of the meetings here in the barn we had turned off almost all of the lights as we prayed and sang praises to the Lord. Two people had a vision of someone standing before the people. Neither of the two knew the other had seen the vision. Neither understood what the vision was all about, but both were told to tell me about it and I would know what it meant. What they saw was a man naked from the waist up with his arms stretched out to each side. They could not see his head or face or his hands. Both came to me afterwards and shared what they had seen. They asked "What does it mean? God told us you would know." I responded: "I have no idea, but if I'm supposed to know God will tell me in His own time." (Now it's beginning to hail outside as the rain continues hard and lightening and thunder is intense; what a hoot). It was several weeks later before I understood the vision.

One night weeks later I was awakened from sleep quite suddenly and I heard what sounded like thousands of bees. The Lord spoke to my heart "What do you hear?" "Bees" I said "thousand of them." "What are they?" he asked. I knew and said "Demons, thousands of them coming upon earth." "That's right" said the Lord and I watched as He put his fists together and came down upon that flood of bees. They splashed like water and separated into two waves. As they did so they formed those two arms that the two people had seen in the barn. I saw the whole picture. The arms were the arms of Satan and two mighty angels were holding them out on each side. They had not seen a face in their vision, but I saw the angry face of Satan. Again God spoke: "I declare to you the nakedness of Satan. His hate is perfect. You cannot make agreements with it. He is a perfect liar. The truth is not him. He will deceive any who forsake the truth." I could see in Scripture that all this was true, but the next statement He made I don't fully understand. God continued: "He is jealous because Jesus has the place in your heart that he would have had if he had not have fallen." I cannot prove that last statement from Scripture and I leave it to the reader to decide what to do with it. During this season God was teaching us a lot about Satan and demons and this was certainly a part of our learning. Could it be that Satan will finally get his desire to live in a human being when he finally inhabits the coming anti-Christ?

It was about this time that I had my first encounter with casting out a demon. As I was leaving for work one morning, I was strongly impressed to pray and fast during the day. Since my work was physically strenuous, I declined fasting, but continued to pray. As the day went on I felt stronger and stronger the need of fasting and by the time I got home it was very intense. I told Peggy I was not eating supper, but was going upstairs to pray. As I prayed it became revealed to me that I was to cast a demon out of a young lady that evening. Even as I was praying I heard the door bell and rushed down to meet a couple of brothers. Before they even told me anything I asked "Who is it and where is she?" They were shocked at my question, but led me to the home where they had been trying to free this girl from demonic possession. They were holding her down. I told them "Let her go, if we can't control her with the power of Jesus, we have no business being here." They let her loose. She told me later (after an hour of deliverance) that she remembered me coming in the door and everything in her wanted to kill me. That was the last thing she remembered as the demon moved to the front and defied our efforts.

I hate casting out demons. I've never been trained to do so. I've had no education in the ritual. I only knew that Jesus is more powerful than all the forces of darkness and I stood against this power in His authority. I guess we learn as we go and eventually we just recognized that the demon had no right to be there in the presence of Jesus and we simply commanded him to go and he went . . . so simple after an hour of sweating it out and trying all the tricks we had ever heard.

I was listening to the news one day and a report came across about a young man that stripped down naked and walked into a department store to visit his girl-friend. Needless to say the police were called and the fellow fled. A car chase followed with the police chasing him across the city of Decatur. He ended up driving off into Lake Decatur in an attempt to drown himself before the police finally apprehended him. As I listened to the news report I made the comment: "that young man is demon possessed." Then I heard the whisper of God "Yes he is and you are going to cast that demon out of him." I shrugged it off and thought "I'm not going to Decatur to try and find him." A day or two later I got a phone call from a brother in a city about an hour South. John said "Bob I need your help. I have a young man in my living room who I think is demon possessed." He told me the story of the young man and it was the same one as in the news report. That deliverance and several more afterwards were a bit easier, but I still don't like doing exorcisms. I have also found that leading people to Jesus and getting them filled with his love, joy, faith and assurance does a lot more good than casting out demonic forces.

John and I had other interesting experiences during this time period. He called me one day to go with him to take some needed food to a family living out in the country. When we arrived there were several cars there. What we discovered when we took the groceries to the door was a full-fledged Satan worship going on. A little scary, but we entered the house in the power of Jesus love and began sharing the gospel. Things got intense and some immediately left, not liking the clashing of light and darkness. Early on a little 8-10 year old boy climbed on top of one of those big spools that hold wire that was being used for a table. He began swinging a butcher knife in the air and shouting "Praise be to Satan, praise be to Satan." I got a bit nervous at this point and retired to the bathroom and got on my knees and did some serious praying. When I returned everyone had left except the man and wife and their kids who lived there. John was witnessing to the husband so I turned to witness to the wife. Every time I used the name Jesus she would say "What did you say?" She couldn't hear His name. Under my breath, I commanded the demon to get out of the way and when I mentioned Jesus again she said "Oh, I hear you now." As this man and wife accepted Jesus the little daughter now climbed up on the spool/table and lifted both of her hands toward heaven and shouted "Praise be to Jesus, praise be to Jesus." I knew then the tide had turned and victory was won. John and I had several such experiences during the period of the Jesus Movement.

One day we were in another nearby city and John said "I know a fellow in this town who really needs Jesus. He is deep in the drug world."

I asked "Where does he live?"

John said "I have no idea."

In the leading of the Spirit I said "Pick a street."

"What?" John said.

"Pick a street" I emphatically repeated.

"Okay" he said, hesitated a few and then said "that one." I turned down the street he pointed toward and I said

"Pick a house." He laughed and pointed to one on the left side about the middle of the block. When we walked to the door we noticed a scared man in his twenties peeking out from behind some blinds. Once inside he unfolded a story of how things had gone bad in a drug deal and there was a contract out on his life. After sharing the gospel with him we invited him to go along with us as we believed he would be safe in our presence. We went calling on some other places and he went in with us and sat silently listening. At one place we noticed he had turned rather white and when we got back to the car he said "You just took me to the home of the guy who has the contract on me." Both showed up at the revival meeting we were holding that night and the Lord intervened and brought peace between them. I never knew what was going to happen whenever John called and said "I need you to come and join me in a visit or ministry."

Another time John called me to come down and help him minister to a woman whose husband had left her for another man. She had been left with a young son and two teen-age daughters. Of course she was devastated and we spent some time sharing and praying with her. It was a rather intense time and I was moved with great compassion for her to the point I knelt down and washed her feet with the tears I was shedding. After awhile I left her with John as I made my way throughout the house letting the Lord lead me to discover hidden occult and witchcraft books and literature. I was reaching up in the back of closets and underneath things to pull this stuff out. The mother had told us that one of the teen-age girls was into witchcraft and the other was on fire with Jesus. I made my way down the hall and came to the end with one door on the left and one on the right. The room on the left had a definite feel of darkness and evil. It was literally cold. The door on the right was full of warmth and light. There was no question as to which girl occupied which room. None of the kids were home at the time.

I called for John to join me and he too sensed the difference in the two rooms. I suggested: "You kneel in the room on the right and I'll kneel in the room on the left and let's pray." We joined hands across the hallway and John began to pray. Immediately I felt the darkness coming into and upon me from the room I was in. It became so overwhelming I noticed that John's voice was quickly fading out of my hearing. As I began to squeeze his hand rather desperately, he realized what was happening and began to pray more fervently and louder. He began to rebuke the evil. He commanded demons to depart from the house. For some weird reason back during those times we frequently cast demons out "to the East." I don't know why, it's just something we did. I felt the power of his prayer flowing to and through me as the darkness began to subside and the light and warmth took its place. We agreed together for a complete purging of the house of all evil.

The "rest of the story" came when we got back to John's house. John lived a few miles east of this troubled lady's house and as we pulled into the driveway a half a dozen kids came running up to the car. They had been playing in the yard. They were quite excited as they said "Guess what we saw? Guess what we saw?" They said they saw angels and demons in battle going across the sky. The angels were driving the demons from West to East over the house. Now I know kids can have vivid imaginations, but often God's miracles come by way of "perfect timing." How is it they would see this battle of the spirit world just as John was praying for the demons to be cast into the East? How many times have we all seen things happen "at the perfect time" that has no other explanation than it was a "God thing?" I could tell stories about that all day long.

FIRST MIRACLE AND
A LOT MORE

One of those "perfect timed" miracles happened many years ago. Me, my younger brother, a cousin and a friend built a big boat and took it for the maiden voyage on the Wabash River in Indiana. We put in at one bridge and went upstream several miles, spent the night and came back the next day. We had built the big boat with a removable framework overhead over which we could throw a tarp and keep off the rain or the hot sun. It was quite a "jungle boat." The friend had taken off his watch and hung it on the framework. The way the frame work was constructed it would seem impossible for the watch to come off, but somewhere along the way it had disappeared. The search throughout the boat was futile, so we turned the boat back upstream and began searching every area where we had stopped to explore and swim. After several stops the atmosphere was pretty dark and dismal as we came up empty handed again and again. He had received the watch as a graduation present from his folks and really felt bad at the apparent loss. At one spot he and I had climbed back into the boat as we waited for my brother and cousin who were still searching the nearby beach. I felt so sad for him that I breathed a prayer under my breath and said "God, help Tom find that watch." Immediately I watched Tom reach over the side of the boat and stick his hand in the mud on the bottom of the Wabash River. Up came his hand with some mud and in the midst was that watch. What are the chances? Is there not great significance that it happened immediately after I prayed the prayer? I actually count that as the first miracle I had witnessed, but it certainly has not been the last. They have continued over the years.

The barn had a room off to the South that had been used for the old "hide room." That's where they stored the hides until they sold them back in the days of the "stink plant." We had done nothing with it and it was dirty and full of years of accumulation of junk. We felt a need of a "counseling room" where we could take people aside after an "invitation" and instruct them further in the ways of the Lord. I decided one day when I was away at work that when I got home I was going to begin cleaning up the hide room and turn it into a counseling room. Imagine my surprise when I entered the room at the end of my work day and found the junk all gone, the place cleaned up, a carpet laid on the old wood floor, pictures of Jesus hanging on the wall and a little stool with a candle on it. "Wow" I thought "who did all this?" I found out later my mother and one of her prayer warriors had got the "call" from God to clean up and fix up the room. They did so without any input from me or anyone else that it should be done. Another "God thing" huh?

I remember an interesting prayer meeting in that room at one of the Happenings. There was a teen-age girl who walked with a very noticeable limp. The young zealous (sometimes over-zealous) believers took her to the room and gathered around her to pray for her healing. I walked in about the time the praying started. They were all on their knees and she sat peacefully in the middle. The praying was intense, loud and fervent. Healing was being called for, actually demanded, in Jesus name and she was being told to simply believe. I could feel the pressure on her as if it was up to her to receive her healing. I felt something was out of order but let things go on for awhile. Finally I turned to the girl in the center and asked her. "Do you want to be healed?" She shrugged her shoulders and said "I don't care; I've learned to live with it." Then I sensed the problem. She had no problem accepting herself the way she was, and I'm sure the Lord didn't either. It was the group around her that had the problem. I began praying for them. I prayed they would learn to accept her the way she is and leave any healing to be done or NOT done to God. It was a good time to teach a bit about healing.

I shared the story of Mose's call to go speak to the Israelites in Egypt and to Pharaoh to let them go. After Moses was given all the necessary instructions and even the promise of miracles to confirm his message, he still was reluctant to go. "I am not eloquent, neither before nor since you have spoken to your servant; but I am slow of speech and slow of tongue." (Exo. 4:10,11). God didn't say "call a prayer meeting and pray that you will be healed" as we might have done. What did God say? "Who has made man's mouth?" (Even with impediments). "Who makes the mute, the deaf, the seeing, or the blind? Have not I, the Lord? Now therefore, go, and I will be with your mouth and teach you what you shall say." I'm sure the "name it and claim it" folks have problems with this verse. So does anyone else who thinks that God wants to heal every affliction and disease that comes along. Sometimes God uses afflictions rather than take them away. People like Joni Erickson Tada, Nick Voijic and Dave Reover all testify they struggled with their afflictions. They sought the miracle of healing and total restoration, but God made it clear that He could best do his work for and through them by using their varied handicaps . . . even as he wanted to do with Moses.

I've certainly prayed for healings and miracles, and I've seen a few, but there have been more times I've seen God use the affliction and even death to accomplish His works. More and more I have learned to pray that folks would have the peace of God in their affliction and trust Him to use it until he takes it away. All afflictions, diseases, handicaps and difficulties will disappear at death when we enter the courts of glory. Until then it could be God wants to make His strength perfect in your weakness. (II Cor. 12:9). Paul sought healing and deliverance from his "thorn in the flesh" (whatever it was) but God refused to heal it. "My grace is sufficient for you" were his final word to Paul and Paul learned to "take pleasure in my infirmities."

For 3 years after I had my cancerous prostate removed I had to wear a "Texas" or condom catheter. It was a real bother and I hated it. I asked God to give me back control of my bladder, but month after month went by and He refused to heal me. One day I realized I had not given Him praise for the situation. (I Thess. 5:18 says "In everything give thanks; for this is the will of God in Christ Jesus concerning you.") I thanked Him that day for the bothersome catheter. The next day I no longer needed it as control returned. The healing was totally unexpected as I had learned to live with the bothersome thing. Will God heal every time we praise Him for a sickness, affliction or problem? Absolutely not. God

Himself is steward of His miracles and He alone knows when it will benefit you and His kingdom the most. With or without the miracle of a healing or deliverance we need to learn to always rejoice in the Lord . . . and we certainly need to quit making people feel guilty when they don't get their healing. Sometimes it takes a lot more faith to live with an affliction then to see it healed. Like the kids in that counseling room trying to get their friend healed, we need to accept folks the way they are before we try to heal them and make them like us The Scriptures are full of examples of how God used the afflictions people went through for good. Often the case is today as it was for Joseph and his brothers when he told them "what you meant for evil, God meant for good" (Gen. 50:20).

Our old barn was the center of a lot of preaching, teaching and ministry during those seven years of 50 Holy Happenings. We gave permission to anyone who wanted to get up and share his love and appreciation for the Lord. We were not always well organized. Even though we made up a schedule for the day which included a variety of study groups across the 15 acres, time for volley ball and other sports, meal times and free time. We were open to the moving of the Spirit and He frequently moved in ways completely unexpected. We tried not to interfere in what the Spirit was doing, but to blend with Him in spontaneous ways.

Once while I was preaching in the barn I received a message from God about a sister sitting there before me. Our eyes met and she knew I had a revelation about her. I didn't mention if before the group as I didn't feel it proper to do so. She came to me after the meeting, outside the barn and said "God showed you something about me didn't He?" "Yes He did" I replied. "He showed me you are trying to break up the music group." (Her husband was an active member of a very popular singing group of that era). She broke down in tears and began to cry "It's true, it's true." I consoled her with the words "Don't you think God revealed it to me because he wants to set you free?" She agreed and after prayer and confession to the group the issue was resolved. I've had such revelations several times and have found it's not always best to declare it before the whole group, but to take it to the individual. God is gentle and orders us to be likewise.

THE TRANSFORMED
PRAYER CELLS

One of the seven inspirational points on Agape Acres are the prayer cells. These are two round brick structures down behind the barn. They were the holding tanks for the blood and animal fluids during the days when this was an animal disposal plant. They are about 20' across and about 7-8' tall. Over the years they have grown up in trees and have become like gardens. The Christ Kids of the 70's help me break a hole in the wall to make a doorway. That wasn't easy as it seems the walls were laid up with concrete for mortar and paving brick in two brick thickness. They are very strong to this day and it took a lot of sledge hammer beating to beat the rugged door way as an entrance.

Over the years we have had a number of different seats in them. We used everything from hay bales to logs. A very unique feature of the prayer cells is the acoustics. If you stand right in the middle and talk, or better yet sing, the sound comes right back into your ears from every direction. It's sort of like singing in the shower but with more emphasis.

The second prayer cell is right up against the first one. It's a bit smaller and at one time we had a roof on it, but one of the young people somehow caught it on fire and we decided to leave the roof off and let it grow up in trees as well.

Long before we purchased the property I had come upon these structures when I was out for a walk one day. I climbed up on the outside and looked in and was fascinated at what appeared to be "secret gardens." I even dropped down into the interior and surveyed the trash and brush which we would later clean out. I had no idea at the time that I would someday own this property and convert these old holding tanks into beautiful prayer cells. Remnants of the foul smell were experienced when we sledge-hammered the holes in the walls for doors.

It's always fun to see the reaction you get when you describe how these tanks were once full of rotting blood and fluids. "If you had stood in here 40 years ago you would have been over your head with the foul fluids." We like to describe our lives as comparable to these tanks. Once we were full of filth and stench and when Jesus came in and cleaned us out we became beautiful gardens for his dwelling much like these prayer cells have become today.

A lot of signs wonders and miracles happened within these brick walls during those 7 years of the Jesus Movement and the 50 Holy Happenings we held on the 15 acres. Some stand out in my memory. There was the time that a couple of the brothers came back from Florida and they wanted to come back and pray and praise the Lord in these confines. The 3 of us stood in the middle of the biggest and first cell and after some intense prayer we began to sing joyful praise. We were singing "How Great Thou Art" when a little brown house wren flew in and sat upon a branch not more than foot above our heads. He sang the beautiful melody that God blessed house wrens with. He sang lustily all the way through the 3 verses that we sang just below him. It gave us goose bumps to have this wonderful accompaniment from our feathered friend. That was an unforgettable experience.

Another memory is of a time when 15 or so brothers and sisters had gathered to pray and praise the Lord. After much prayer we began to sing with Tom leading us as he strummed the praises on his guitar. During those days we had a little brown dog named Rex who often joined our group and sat silently listening to our joyful songs. This day he was right in the center of the cell as we were all in a ring around him leaning back against the circular brick wall. Tom, our song leader, paused the singing and made the statement: "you know, I believe if we didn't sing and praise the Lord, that dog would be anointed to do it for us." No sooner were the words out of his mouth than Rex did something I had never seen him do before nor did I ever see him do it after. He laid his head back, looked up to the blue sky and began a warbling bark-like sound for a full 5-10 seconds. We all sat in stunned shock and silence and then broke forth in laughter and praise. A remarkable experience! God once made a donkey speak to the prophet Balaam, so it should not surprise us that He can inspire a dog to praise Him.

Summer and winter folks came and spent time in prayer, praise and meditation in the prayer cells. Day and night they came. Owls could be heard and glow-worms were observed during the nights and the rays of sunshine and the singing of song birds surrounded the place during the day. Over the years flowers have been planted and flourished in the fertile ground. Every spring the floor of the first prayer cell is covered with blooming blue-bells. Dry-land-tortoises have frequented the habitat. It seems there has always been at least one that has made it his permanent home. A perfect setting for prayer, praise and meditation.

People have come here to seek and find Jesus. Once the teen-agers brought the community "girl with a reputation" out and set her down on a bale of hay in the middle of the first cell and told her: "If you'll just sit here Jesus will come to you." I happen to come by later and found Betty sitting on the bale softly crying. When I asked what her problem was she told me what the kids had done and said to her. I gently told her the old Gospel story and she invited Jesus into her life and began the eternal journey of the abundant life. There were others who came and were simply overwhelmed by all that was happening in the lives of the young people of that era and this place became a perfect place to connect with our graceful Savior.

The door to the 2nd prayer cell was made by breaking through the double walls where the two were up against one another. That turned out to be a slow laborious project. It went on for days with different ones coming and beating on the solid brick and concrete until they wore them-selves out. We didn't even try to make a full size door as we had for the entry to the first cell. This entry to the second is only about 4' tall, so you have to humbly bend over to enter. I was beating away at the wall one day and finally got a bit of a hole started. I kept swinging and sweating until I finally got a hole big enough I could crawl through. I was thinking "wow, I'm the first one to make it through the door," even though it was a long ways from a finished doorway. I may have been a bit proud of myself as I crawled through the small hole. At any rate I didn't even get a chance to stand to my feet.

Suddenly I was impressed with the mighty hand of God driving me to fall on my face in the dirt of that second prayer cell. God impressed a message strong and clear upon my heart

"Bob you have never done anyone any good whatsoever."

That message was rather humbling since I thought I had just done a good thing in opening a passage between the two cells. I was impressed with a further message:

"You will never do anyone any good whatsoever."

That drove me even closer to the dirt I lay in, but He wasn't thru.

"Even if you try to do anyone any good, I assure you will do them more harm than good."

That left me utterly broken, crushed, humbled and speechless. Then He gently impressed me with:

"But I have put my Spirit upon you and He has never done anyone any harm whatsoever. He will never do anyone anything but good. And even if He tried to do them harm, He would end up doing them good."

That message was rather comforting, especially following the initial message. Looking at the Scripture in John 15 brings me the assurance that the voice I was hearing was indeed from our heavenly Father. Jesus is the Vine and only if we abide in Him and let His words abide in us will we bear any good fruit, for as he said "apart from Me you can do nothing." That's a message we all need to frequently ponder. Pride is the biggest obstacle to real fruitfulness in the kingdom of God.

Not only have I enjoyed the fellowship with God many times in these confines, I have also wrestled with the powers of darkness. I have had people pull me aside and seek to dissuade me from following what I knew God had placed on my heart. One night I came to the cells alone and as I prayed I felt the cold dark presence of the enemy who sought to turn my faith away from my simple trust in God. After an hour or so of deep struggle I felt the evil presence leave and the sweet Spirit of God came and made my heart overflow with joy, peace, love and an unusual discernment. The experience of that joy and peace is difficult to describe. I seemed to be at a oneness with the universe. I could touch a tree and feel every leaf and heart of the tree beneath the bark. It was strange, but very peaceful. I don't try to understand every experience I've had with God. It was what it was and my love and appreciation of His love and grace only increased.

Are there times and places where God is more predominant? I don't know. Did Jesus frequent any place? Yes, it seems the Garden of Gethsemane was such a place. I know strange and wonderful things happened all over Agape Acres during those 7 years and people were blessed beyond natural explanation at the time. God used a rooster to convict Peter and a donkey to rebuke the erring prophet so we should not be surprised that He can use a round brick structure once used to hold blood and guts to transform the lives of people to joy, peace and love. He certainly did it here time and again.

I can't explain why some things happened the way they did here. I simply tell you what I've seen and heard and what others have told me they saw and heard. You can draw your own conclusions. For example, at one of the early Happenings my sister-in-law Geneva made her way down to the prayer cells. She had heard how people were blessed by going there and praying and singing. She circled the cells, but could see no door (it is very evident). Later after a meeting in the barn we were all going to the cells to pray. She told Stan, her husband, she didn't really want to go. She had seen a small ladder that was leaning up against the wall and she thought people would be climbing that ladder to get in. This trip down she did see the door and told Stan "that was not there earlier in the day." As we gathered for prayer and praise she also looked up and saw a wall of fire all around the outside of the prayer cell. What did it mean? What was God trying to teach us? You figure it out.

THE INTRIGUING BAPTISTERY
AND BAPTISMS

The creek that flows in the back of the property is quite small. It's not much more than ankle deep in most places. However, there is one spot in the creek where it's a bit deeper. One day we decided to make that spot into a baptistery. Before that we had baptized several in the Oakland Lake and down the road in the Little Embarrass River. John and Jerry joined in helping me make a small dam and digging the hole until it was about waist deep. After a few hours of work we felt it was suitable and joined hands in the cold water and prayed that God would send folks to be baptized.

We made the quarter mile walk back to the house and a young fellow was sitting in his car waiting on us. "I want to be baptized" he told us. He was our first. While we were baptizing him my younger brother and his wife showed up saying "we want to be baptized." Within the hour we had baptized three and over the months and years following we baptized hundreds in that little pool. (The water was always cold as it seems to be spring fed.). A 3 trunk willow tree grew up beside the pool of water and it became dubbed "Trinity Tree" and gave rise to some teachings on the "3 in 1" theology. (An interesting "Rest of the story" incident came some 40 years after that first baptism: I was attending a rather large church in a neighboring city recently when this fellow began attending there as well. One day I discovered an old booklet of baptismal certificates. His was still in there with the date he was baptized. I took it to church and brought a pleasant surprise to him when I handed it to him.)

A sizable crowd had gathered on the hill-side overlooking the baptistery one cool fall day as we prepared to baptize several. As usual I took the time to do a little teaching before entering the water to baptize the candidates. The birds had gathered in the surrounding trees in their fall migration and were raising a loud ruckus. It seemed only natural to wave my arm at them and loudly command "PEACE, BE STILL." They hushed instantly and I went ahead teaching. When I finished my message I turned back to the waiting birds and said "Okay, I'm done." Instantly they went back to their noisy chattering. I didn't take it as a miracle at the time because it just seemed the natural/normal thing to do.

A pastor from a nearby town was sitting on the hill-side and witnessed that strange scene. He was awe-struck at the "bird miracle." He later told how it was repulsive for him to watch those people go down into that muddy little pool of cold water. He cringed at the thought of mud squeezing up between their toes. We would later discover the ministerial association of that city had commissioned him to come and do an investigation of what was going on at this place called "Agape Acres." He spent the day in his fancy suit wandering in and out of meetings in the barn, prayer cell, and other spots on the property. I did notice he got a bit stiff when I gave him the customary "agape hug" when I greeted him. It was not until the last meeting in the barn that day that all this came out. He stood before the group and told why he was there and how he had reacted to the baptisms and the strange activity of the birds. Then he said "I find no fault in what is going on here, in fact whatever you folks have found, I want to be part of it. Not only that, but God has convicted me that I need to be baptized in that muddy water and have the mud squeeze up between my toes." We did so that evening in the darkening evening as the kids from his church sang for joy. The brother became a Spirit-filled servant of God which eventually got him dismissed from his rather staid and "stiff" church, but he went on to years of successful ministry before the Lord called him home. He and his wife had a good ministry together and his children followed suit.

I have no idea how many hundreds were baptized in that little creek. Sometimes it was the kids who became obedient to their Lord and sometimes it was their leaders. Parents and other adults who came to investigate were caught up by the influence of the Holy Spirit and wanted to be prayed for and baptized as they committed or re-committed themselves to the Lord. Those were glorious times indeed. I just recently reconnected to a sister on facebook who told me she came here when she was but 10 and remembers one evening after a meeting when we baptized 15 people. That may have been the one where the birds were put to silence. My brother told how the water was so cold sometimes that his jaws would lock up and he couldn't even speak as he baptized several. We kept no records of how many and who all were baptized during those years. God alone knows and He is the only one who really needs to know.

Probably a dozen weddings took place in many different places across the property. I do remember at least two took place on the banks of the baptistery beneath the old "Trinity Tree."

Baptism (especially by immersion) is a beautiful picture of how we are to die to self and be buried with Jesus. We are then raised with Him as He came out of the grave and we now have eternal life with Him. Baptism does not save, but faith in what He did for us in suffering, dying, being buried and raised does. Baptism identifies us as those who believe that gospel. Although I don't believe baptism saves, I see no reason why anyone would refuse to obey their Lord and Savior in this beautiful ritual. I often compare it to the wedding ring. The ring does not make you married, but it is a beautiful endless circle that demonstrates marriage is meant to last a life-time. Refusing to be baptized would be like refusing to wear the ring of your beloved mate.

One of the most intriguing stories I have ever heard about baptism took place in a small church in a big city not far from here. The candidate had accepted Jesus and they were trying to explain to her the meaning behind baptism. There was a real communication problem as she was of foreign origin and did not fully understand the explanation. They did notice she was very reluctant to be baptized, and even trembled as they led her down into the waters. However, when she came up she came up shouting for joy. As a clearer understanding came out as they continued to struggle with communication it was discovered that she thought they were going to literally drown her . . . this she took from being told she was "dying with Christ." She believed that she would be raised and brought back to life. Wow. Would you consent to be baptized if you believed that was what they were going to do to you? This sister had faith.

One of my most memorable baptisms was the day I baptized my son Timothy. He was in high school at the time. I woke him up a bit early that day and said "You're not going to school today. Today Agape Acres belongs to just you and me." He shouted "Praise God" as he rolled out of bed and proceeded to get dressed. I had not given him, or my two daughters, the time and attention I should have during those times. I was so wrapped up in reaching out to all the other teens that came to the property that I honestly neglected spending the time with my own kids that I should have. He was thrilled that I had set aside this day for just me and him.

After breakfast we walked around the property and left word with his mother to tell people we really didn't want any other company to interrupt us. We shared the things of God back in the barn, down in the prayer cells and down by Andrew's cross. He decided he wanted to be baptized so we went to the hole in the creek by Trinity Tree. We both went down into the cold water and I baptized him in the name of the Father, the Son and the Holy Ghost. It was a special time for both of us. Many ministers have often neglected their own families in their noble efforts to try to reach the suffering, dying and lost world around them. That is a big mistake. One's family should be a minister's first team-mates in rescuing the perishing. I did struggle with that over the years.

ANDREW'S CROSS

During our 2nd Holy Happening here on the property some of the young people from a nearby large town brought this 20' cross to our property. They had held a youth rally in a city park there and had stood the cross up as part of the rally. When they were done the city demanded that they remove the cross. The question came to mind "What do we do with an abandoned cross?" Someone suggested bringing it to Agape Acres and put it back up there somewhere.

"Where would you like to have it?" they asked.

I knew just the place. "Follow me"

They carried it back a winding trail across the creek, past the baptistery and Trinity Tree to a location in the NE section of the 15 acres. There it stands to this day. (My son-in-law keeps the trail and the 30' circle around the cross mowed.) I don't know exactly when we named it "Andrew's Cross." It could have been the day we stood it up or perhaps very shortly thereafter, but the name stuck. Three Andrew's inspired the name. The first was Peter's brother Andrew who led Peter to Jesus. We have taken this Andrew as an example of how we should also lead people to the Lord, especially family members.

The second Andrew was a fellow called "Brother Andrew." He was at the time heavily engaged in smuggling Bibles into countries closed to such a practice. The cross was to remind us to pray for him and those who carry on such a dangerous ministry, as well as to pray for all those living in such countries. Brother Andrew's ministry continues to this day.

The third Andrew was a baby boy born the day we stood the cross up. (He must be about 40 years old today.) We knew nothing of that birth until sometime later. His parents had attended meetings with us during these years and at one time Andrew's dad met "the need of the hour." We were preparing to take a couple of car-loads of teens to Florida for a week-long seminar on personal witnessing which would include going out on Daytona Beach to do actual witnessing (at which several accepted Jesus as personal Savior). A day or two before we were to leave we had gathered around our huge dining table to discuss and pray about how to raise the necessary funds. We were still short a few hundred dollars from the needed amount. We had written the exact amount needed on a slip of paper and placed it in the center of the table, and we then prayed over it.

After we finished praying there was a knock at the door. It was Andrew's dad. He came in and said

"I heard you were taking a bunch of kids to Florida. Do you have all the money you need for the trip?"

"No, we do not. In fact we have just prayed for God to supply it."

He sat down at the table and wrote out a check and handed it to me. I smiled when I looked at it and handed it to the kids standing around. They smiled as well. Then I picked up the slip of paper lying in the middle of the table, turned it over and handed it to Andrew's dad. You guessed it . . . the check was for the exact amount as written on the piece of paper. God has confirmed our ministry over and over in just such manners. How good of Him.

It was during this 2nd Happening that we baptized several more young people in the Oakland Lake. We also loaded all the kids on hay wagons and took them to a tent revival being held in Oakland. The porn-burning was also held during this 2nd happening.

At our third Holy Happening we came up with a theme of "Total Commitment to Jesus Christ." As part of the expression of that week-end we encouraged the kids (and several adults) to come down to Andrew's cross and nail up a little white flag when they understood and became convinced that they wanted to fully surrender their lives to the guidance of Jesus. As we taught lessons on that theme all week-end the cross became more and more covered with those little white flags.

(Many of the small nails are still in the cross although over the years all traces of the flag material are gone). Some nailed them as high as they could reach (one boy even scaled the pole and nailed his on the cross piece). Others nailed theirs at the very bottom. I reckon each one was trying to make an expression of his commitment. One hopes that the commitments made that week-end have lasted longer than the little flags that have deteriorated away. 6 more of the kids were baptized in Lake Oakland as an expression of their total commitment to the Christ they had come to love.

At that same Happening someone had brought in a bunch of watermelons for the crowd to feast on. People gathered around to look them over in the back of the donor's truck. After unloading them and placing them in the shape of a cross on the ground someone suggested:

"Let's take them down to Andrew's Cross and pray over them." Those who had helped unload them each picked one up to carry down the trail. One little boy was discovered crying as he struggled to carry his watermelon to the cross. Someone asked him:

"Why are you crying?"

"I can barely carry it down here. When the Lord blesses it and makes it bigger, I won't be able to carry it back."

Ah, for the faith of a child. We could surely change the world.

Another time I led several kids down to the cross for a prayer meeting about some matter that was upon one of their hearts. These kids tended to get very excited when they talked to the Lord during those years. The prayer meeting soon turned into shouts of praise and then they began to ask the Lord to come down and take them home right now. They were begging Him to do it NOW. I had joined in with them until I felt the gentle nudge from the Lord.

"Do you really want me to come and get you now Bob? I can pass over the over-exuberance of these kids, but I take you a bit more serious."

I slowly backed out of the circle and shut my mouth leaving them to continue their zealous shouts for deliverance from mother earth. I preferred to wait and go another day when more ministry had been performed.

I remember at least two weddings at the cross. It is a beautiful spot surrounded by tall trees, singing birds and the green decorations of carpeting and ceiling. I was a bit surprised at one young couple who showed up for their wedding in full formal attire, including a sweeping long white dress on the beautiful bride. It had rained all night and needless to say the trail was a bit muddy. I pointed this out thinking they might want to change their minds, but they gave me to know it didn't matter. The wedding went on . . . dirty white train and all. Perhaps more marriages would last longer if folks didn't get bent out of shape over a little dirt that often accumulates along the way.

One of the more spectacular events I witnessed at Andrew's was that involving a young man named Ted. Ted was a member of a Gospel Rock group and had a reputation of being a bit on the wild side, but nonetheless a believer. Standing around the barn one day someone told him if he would run down to Andrew's cross God would give him a special blessing. I happened to be sitting on the hillside above the baptistery sharing with the young sister from France when Ted went bounding by in a big hurry. Of course we wondered what his rush was all about, but didn't give it much thought; at least not until we heard him coming back up the trail shouting as he ran just as fast back up as he had when he ran down. He had fallen on his knees at the cross and waited for God to bless him. His expectations were not in vain. It was a rather calm, but partly cloudy day. Suddenly a small cloud came over the cross with a bit of a whirl-wind and released a flood of rain-drops that drenched the waiting teen. It was the only spot on the property to get any rain that day. As he ran back up the hill he was shouting "The Lord just baptized me. The Lord just baptized me." As I've said before, I don't try to analyze these experiences, I am just telling what I have seen and heard. Perhaps Ted needed something a bit extraordinary to reach into his somewhat compromised life. God knows what each of us needs and when we need it.

Taking the Message out to the Churches

I was thrilled with the way God was rescuing kids right off the streets. They were coming into the kingdom still wearing ear rings, long hair, tattoos and bib overalls, but their joy peace and love were contagious. Jesus had become everything to them and they were ready to shout from the house tops how good He is. I thought "if only the churches could see this zeal they would appreciate these kids." With that thought in mind I took 6 of these young men to a nearby country church. I thought their smiles, hugs, handshakes and good words would bless the people and open their eyes to what God was doing with the Jesus Movement. Everything went fine until the preacher happened to say "Does anyone here today have a good word for their Lord and Savior?" "Uh oh" I thought, "here we go." These six guys rose to their feet and took the next 20 minutes or so giving him an answer to his question. The preacher was a bit nervous, but he let them have their say. He got a bit more nervous as several of the old folks rose to their feet and exited the building. When we got back to the car I found a note taped to my steering wheel that read "Don't bring that riff-raff back to our church." It broke my heart that they could not see a work of God right in front of their noses. Tradition is a hard thing to battle and closes the minds of people from seeing the pathway that God would love to take folks down. No, I never took the boys back there again.

Some new fellowship/churches sprung up in the area and across the nation. I started attending one in a nearby town. Some unorthodox, but good things were happening there. One Sunday I felt led to make up communion bread. I baked a round piece of pie crust and took it with me. Another person felt lead to bring a plate and my crust fit perfectly down into the recessed plate. Another brought wine and another a cup. None of us knew that the others were bringing their respective parts to what developed into a great communion service. Healings and deliverances came into that meeting and dancing with great joy.

One fellow was brought in possessed of demons. His face was covered with flies and you could brush them off, but they would come right back on. (Is there significance that "Beelzebub" means "Lord of the flies?") When we cast the demon out the flies left him. Another fellow came in with bad welder burn in his eyes. I knew the pain because I had the same thing several years before and it was hours before it wore off. We prayed for him and he was instantly healed. When we break with our traditional, human ways of doing things we can expect God to do "great and mighty things we know not." (Jer. 33:3).

Another strange thing happened one night. Our daughter and her first husband (who was later killed in a car accident) had moved in with us for a season as they struggled with finances. He was not fully surrendered to the Lord yet, but was coming around. After my wife and I had prayed together I turned out the light, lay back in bed with the intention of going to sleep. Suddenly a Scripture verse began to repeat over and over in my head: Isaiah 42:25. I tried to think of what it was, but couldn't recall. It would not go away so I finally turned on the light and reached for my Bible. I opened it and read: "Therefore He has poured on him the fury of His anger and the strength of battle; It has set him on fire all around, yet he did not know; and it burned him, yet he did not take it to heart." "What in the world is that supposed to mean" I thought as I closed the Bible, turned out the light and went to sleep.

In the middle of the night my daughter came screaming into our bedroom "The house is on fire." Her husband had fallen asleep smoking and set their bed on fire. It had burned "all around" them and left them virtually untouched. After we put out the fire with a bit of battle I set them down and shared what I had received earlier from the Scripture. Eventually he did receive the Lord, was baptized and it's my hope to be reunited with him in glory. God does work in mysterious ways.

THE PAVILION

As the ministry grew here on Agape Acres and more and more folks started coming we saw the need of a facility that would house a kitchen to feed the multitude and bathrooms to handle the growing needs. In the beginning most of our meetings were in the barn and we ate our meals in our home. We filed people in the back-door and out the front and they filled their plates and sat around in the yard. Seeing the need for better facilities we decided to build a pavilion equipped with two bathrooms and a complete kitchen with about double everything: 2 sinks, 2 stoves, 2 fridges, etc. It was all done with volunteer help and funds. It ended up being a closed in facility about 30' wide by 60' long. We made several big picnic tables and finally got people out of the rain and eventually closed it in and had them in out of the cold. We built a huge fireplace at one end opposite of where the kitchen/bathroom complex stood. All this construction was done with volunteer help and donations. All the cooking was done by volunteers with our mother doing the supervising. There was always "joy unspeakable and full of glory" taking place in that busy kitchen as they prepared meals for upwards of 200 people. One sister tells of how they were running out of iced tea and mom told her to just keep pouring. It became the "pitcher that never ran dry." Another time when money was needed to pick up more groceries, a twenty dollar bill appeared in the trash. It served us well over the years until it burnt down some time back in the 80's. We built a home where it had stood and today my daughter and her husband live there in the middle of the woods.

We battled to keep fresh water flowing to the place. Before we got the well hooked up we had a huge water wagon parked behind the place and fed water in by the bucket for both the bathrooms and the kitchen. We had a good well, but it was old and had filled with mud over the years and slowed down the flow of the vein. I volunteered to go down inside and bucket the mud out. I was clothed in a rain-coat and hard hat to protect from drippings and rocks as they pulled bucket after bucket up after I scooped them full. I was using post-hole diggers to do the digging. The more I took out the faster the water began to flow in. They lowered a pump down, but after awhile it could not keep up with the growing flow. At one point I took the post-hole-jobbers and started shoving them down into the middle of the well. The bottom had "quickened" and the jobbers just wanted to keep on going toward the center of the earth. I yelled at my helpers above "Get me out of here; the bottom is turning to quicksand." That old well has never run dry. The flow is strong enough that once when we were gone for the week-end the pipes in the pavilion froze and burst. A ¾ inch water line ran continuously all week-end and never run the well dry, but a frozen waterfall formed on the outside that was 3' thick.

The showers came in handy on hot summer days. Also one time there was a sister who apparently saw no need of taking baths. To put it mildly, she stunk. Several of the caring sisters cornered her and said "You are taking a shower . . . now." She did and was much more pleasant to be around. My son and his wife were the first to be married in the completed pavilion. For awhile we held church services in the dining room as we gathered each Sunday morning around the newly laid up fire-place. After one such service we had left a warm cozy fire blazing in the fire-place and left to go somewhere for the rest of the day. A young married couple showed up after we had all left. They had come to talk with me and share that they wanted to get a divorce. Finding themselves alone they sat in front of the fireplace and God put their relationship back on the right track. Sometimes the property itself was all that people needed. That and the constant presence of God.

Many good things happened in and around the pavilion especially during inclement weather. Whenever weather allowed we still loved to meet in the old barn. Years after the Jesus Movement had faded and folks had quit coming we decided to turn the facility into our home and give our house to our daughter and her husband and 2 kids.

Unfortunately a fire broke out and the pavilion was a total loss. That was depressing, but standing among the ashes I was able to praise God for whatever He was teaching us, and for whatever He had in mind for the future.

Like in the barn the kids brought their guitars and a heart full of love for Jesus. They sang songs and shared their testimonies of good things the Lord had done for them. They joined with other young people and formed groups that went out to area churches and shared God's love and the Gospel. Things didn't just happen here on the property, far to the contrary, the good news spread all over the area and even the world.

One time I took a couple of car loads to a church camp where teens from area churches had gathered for a week of camping. Our kids shared the joy and zeal they had for Jesus. We hoped it would be contagious, but this group of kids at this camp were dead in their seats. There was just no good response to our kid's ministry. They were a little let down at the lack of response, but I encouraged them to believe they had sown good seed and leave it to God to bring forth fruit in due season.

What we didn't know, but found out several weeks later was what happened the night after we left the camp. The kids had all gone to bed quietly and one of the camp counselors was awakened in the night by the sound of one of the kids crying. She went to the girl and asked what her problem was. She said between sobs: "I want what those kids have that shared with us tonight." Soon the whole dorm was awake and up wanting the same thing. The boy's dorm was also stirred and in the middle of the night they all got up and went to the chapel and had a very tear-filled revival. How glad our kids were when they heard their labors were not in vain.

We went out to many churches and schools spreading God's joy and love. Several of the kids had formed a very successful musical group called "Agape Union." Although they had all moved to Florida and were ministering there, I booked them for two weeks in our area. During the day they shared at a local school and in the evening they shared in a local church in different cities all over East Central Illinois. Many kids were saved and spurred to zeal by this ministry. The group had a falling out in the middle of the two weeks and almost gave up the series.

I had planned one day off where they spent a night and day on a cabin at a lake and during that time they patched things up among them and went on to a 2nd week of success. On the last night of the series they had just finished up a concert in a Methodist church when the huge sound board suddenly went up in smoke. God had kept it going up to the last minute and they were able to praise Him for His constant care.

On one occasion we built a huge bon-fire to burn all the witch-craft books, suggestive music, and whatever else the kids felt stood between them and Jesus. It surprised us when one young fellow tossed his 12 string guitar in the fire. He testified that it was making him arrogant and carnal. One young fellow had me go with him behind the pavilion to witness his devotion to the Lord by taking a hammer to his transistor radio. Did these guys need to do this? Who am I to say? The rich young ruler was told by Jesus to sell everything he had, give it to the poor and come follow Him. Not everyone was told to do that, but if God tells you to do it, you better if you want God's best. These young men believed God drew them a little closer to Himself by their sacrifices. What is there in your life or mine that we should consider giving up?

Today we have rebuilt a home upon the foundation left behind from the fire. It is a five-bedroom home with two baths, an enlarged kitchen and a huge family room where my daughter, her husband and I live. The place continues to be a blessing to our family and other folks who come to visit the property and us.

Time certainly changes all things temporal, material and physical. Although God is the "same yesterday, today and forever" that's not true of us and our environment. Just as much as the property and buildings have changed, so have we and our bodies. At one time we mowed all of the property except what was on the East side of the little creek. We never knew exactly how much to mow. I remember thinking "God, I don't know how to handle a blade of grass on this property, let alone these hundreds of young people." We had to trust Him to provide for all the needs, and He did. Today, much of the property is left wild for the deer, squirrels, rabbits and other wild life. We have enjoyed the place and the people at all the various stages over the years. This is the only place our 40 grand-kids have ever known us to live, and they have all had their fun times on every one of the 15 acres in all their child-hood antics.

PART FOUR

30 years of bondage in sin

WARNING DREAMS AND THE
BEGINNING OF THE FALL

Although we were having great times and successful ministry over those 7 years, there were indications that something was brewing in the dark works of the enemy. My mother and I both had dreams that suggested something not so good was developing. She dreamed of a 3-headed snake stretching nearly 30' from our front door to the kitchen. It was a scary creature. She said I had captured the thing and was holding it just back of the heads as they were trying their best to bite me. She said I showed no fear even though one of the heads was even more vicious than the others. She said she could hear my dad shouting in the back-ground "Kill it, Kill it, Kill it." The dream scared her but I assured her not to worry about it.

Then I had what I believe was a dream with significance. I was standing behind the old home place where I grew up. Before me was the garden we raised vegetables in. In the middle of the garden was a beautiful majestic bird. He was as tall as a man and was as colorful and pretty as a cock pheasant. I drew near to him to look him over and as I got close enough I realized he was evil because I could see it in his eyes. Not only were his eyes evil but they were magnetic and were drawing me closer to him so he could destroy me. I noticed that his beak came out in 3 sharp points and I also knew I needed to break his spell and run. I finally did and as I ran up the hill he began to shoot 3-pointed spears at me from his 3-pointed beak. The spears were sticking in the ground all around me. Suddenly I realized he was Satan and I told myself. "I don't have to fear him. Jesus has given me power over all his power." As I stopped and turned to face him he shot a spear directly at my face. I reached up and grabbed it just before it hit me. Then he released a volley of spears and I used the spear in my hand to knock all of them aside. As I gained courage I began to advance on him. When he saw I had lost my fear I saw fear come into his eyes. He began to run for cover under deep grass that was folded over near by. As he darted under the grass I leaped on top of it and began jabbing the spear all over with the hopes of nailing him down. He came out some distance away and flew off.

I now believe God was showing me by these two dreams and the word that he would later give me on the step between my kitchen and dining room that I was about to go into a very deep season of trial. I had no idea it would last as long as it would and just how severe that trial would be, but I was about to find out.

GOD'S PROMISE "I WILL TAKE YOU THROUGH"

Even while we were still in the midst of great things happening at Agape Acres during those 7 years of the early 70's, the enemy had begun to pull me down. Just prior to a "great falling away" God had set me down on the step between our living room and kitchen and spoke clearly to my heart:

"Bob, I'm going to take you through a Red Sea, I'm going to take you through a lion's den, I'm going to take you through a fiery furnace . . . but hear Me, I'm going to take you T H R O U G H!!"

I would need to be reminded of those warning but reassuring words many times in the coming 30 years of bondage. I was about to slip into a life of adultery, sensual sexual sin, debauchery, disobedience, deception and lies. Those years would destroy my marriage, deeply hurt my family, threaten my health, and quench the work of the Spirit in my life. As deep as I would sink, it would not be so low that God would forsake me. He walked with me through those years just as He promised "I will never leave you nor forsake you." Heb. 13:5. Like the straying prodigal, I had "lost my senses." Like Nebuchadnezzar I had the mind of an animal, but my "season" was 30 instead of 7 as in his case.

More than once I seriously considered suicide, but every time I sunk that low the Lord was there to tell me "Bob I promised you I would walk you THROUGH this. I love you. I won't fail you. Trust me to get you through."

I tried again and again to break the chains that bound me. I put a canoe in the river and spent 10 days trying to float away from myself which was proven futile. I spent 6 weeks in the mountains hoping that the change of scenery would change something inside me. I ran as far South as Key West and sought to fling my weaknesses into the gulf at the Southern-most point in the U.S. Nothing seem to help. Every time I returned home it was the same thing all over again. I fought off depression, anger, fear, doubt.

I even tried to just give in to the compulsions and run after any woman that was available. God miraculously stopped any effort in that direction. I couldn't get any better, but neither would God let me get any worse. It's like He was saying "You'll go this far, but no farther."

I found an SAA group (Sex Addicts Anonymous). Although the 12-step group did not give me complete freedom, it did bring new light and hope. For the first time I found a group that accepted me just as I am. I could tell them my whole story . . . even stuff that I did as a kid when I played with the neighbor girls and even a homosexual fling with a friend. They did not judge, condemn or try to straighten me out. They let me work my own program without putting any pressure on me. They were persuaded that my "higher power" could and would lead me to freedom as I got honest with Him and trusted in Him. I made it no secret that my higher power was none other than Jesus Christ.

Over the years I found a few individuals that I could be completely honest with. One fellow was struggling with the same sin and insanity that I was wrestling with. We became accountable to each other and that was a great help.

I fathered 5 children by this partner . . . one was a miscarriage. Finally I made up my mind to divorce my wife and marry this woman. As much as I tried to make that happen, God threw road-block after road-block in that pathway. When it became evident that was not going to happen I think I hit my lowest point. I felt like a man who had gone under the water for the third time and I barely had my nose out of the water. Yet, as low as I was, I sensed the faithfulness of my God and Savior who continued to repeat "I promised you I would take you through this, and I am." I only survived that long 30 years by the great grace and faithfulness of God. Left to myself I would have ended my life or lost my faith in that raging battle.

I've had people tell me that I could not have possibly been saved during that time. I don't agree with them. We are not saved by our good works; neither are we lost because of our bad performance. "For by grace you have been saved through faith, and that not of yourselves; it is the gift of God, not of works, lest anyone should boast." Eph. 2:8. I never stopped believing that. I continually confessed and grieved over my failure: "If we confess our sins, He is faithful and just to forgive us our sins and to cleanse us from all unrighteousness." God didn't put a time line on that. Some folks think the cleansing has to be immediate, but life does not play out that way. I think the success of 12-step recovery works well because they give people time to heal. It's not forced. They just expect you to be honest, real and authentic. Day after day, year after year I kept coming to the foot of the cross and laying my helpless soul before His great grace and again and again He whispered to my troubled soul: "I love you; I am walking you THROUGH this."

THE WIRE ON MY WALL

God gave me a strong sign of confirmation of His faithfulness during those troublesome years. I was hauling something in my pick-up truck going up route 130. I was fretting, worrying, anxious and praying about all the tangles going on in my life. I glanced in the rear-view mirror and noticed my tail-gate was down. Not wanting to have what I was hauling to fall out I pulled over on the shoulder to shut the gate. God reminded me there are no accidents in the life of His children and I should see this small interruption as something for my benefit. Sarcastically I said "Yeah, I suppose there is a bag of money laying out there." That would at least solve some of my financial problems. As I slammed the tail-gate shut I looked down in the grass and gravel and noticed a mass of tangled and smashed baling wire. I thought "yeah, that looks like my tangled and messed up life. Thanks for the reminder God" I continued my sarcasm. As I slipped back into my truck the Lord spoke to my heart "Take another look at the tangle of wire." I looked back and noticed that in the midst of the tangle there was one straight wire that went through it all. He spoke again "And I have promised to take you THROUGH and I will." For the next hour I meditated and rejoiced on God's promises "I will never leave you nor forsake you" Heb. 13:5; "Lo, I am with you always, even to the end of the age" Matt. 28:20; "Fear not, for I am with you; be not dismayed, for I am your God. I will strengthen you, yes, I will help you, I will uphold you with My righteous right hand" Isa. 41:10. Many other affirming Scriptures rolled around in my memory.

Much later in the day, on my return home I passed by where the wire was. I stopped and ran across the highway to pick up the wire and take it home. It had a neat hook just like a coat hanger by which to hang it up. As I was carrying it back to the truck the straight wire fell out in the middle of the highway. Again the Lord spoke to my heart "Someday I will deliver you completely out of all these twists and tangles you suffer in this world." I picked the straight piece up and weaved it back through the tangle and today that wire hangs on my wall. It has been a great reminder of the faithfulness of God over 35 years. Don't get me wrong. I don't rely on such rather weird experiences to affirm my faith. God's word is my guide, but I have found that He uses many such "signs and wonders" to confirm His promises.

A similar "confirmation" came one day when I looked out our dining room window and noticed a little bird had somehow made his way into the bird feeder. I could see him behind the glass front desperately beating his wings against the glass to get out. I was moved with sympathy and went out, opened the top and let the little critter go free. As I walked back to the house the Lord spoke to my heart "you had compassion on that little bird and set him free. Do you not understand that I have greater compassion for you and I WILL set you free from the bondage you suffer?" I love the ways God deals with us in intimate and very personal ways. He is so good. I repeat, it's the Scriptures that bear out the truth and faithfulness of God. One of my favorite passages that has given me hope time and again is found in Romans 8:31-39 "What then shall we say to these things? If God is for us, who can be against us? He who did not spare His own Son, but delivered Him up for us all, how shall He not with Him also freely give us all things? Who shall bring a charge against God's elect? It is God who justifies. Who is he who condemns? It is Christ who died, and furthermore is also risen, who is even at the right hand of God, who also makes intercession for us. Who shall separate us from the love of Christ? Shall tribulation, or distress, or persecution, or famine, or nakedness, or peril, or sword? As it is written: 'for your sake we are killed all day long; we are accounted as sheep for the slaughter. Yet in all these things we are more than conquerors through Him who loved us. For I am persuaded that neither death nor life, nor angels nor principalities nor powers, nor things present nor things to come, nor height nor depth, nor any other created thing, shall be able to separate us from the love of God which is in Christ Jesus our Lord."

Some good times during the bad time

God did not forsake me or set me idle on the shelf during those 30 years. Every Saturday I would go to town to have breakfast with my mother. We did this for the last five years of her life and I really miss those good times. We would study the Bible together and pray over all the concerns in the family. They were great times. One time as I was heading in there I came up to the highway and noticed a young couple hitch-hiking in the opposite direction of where I was going. I heard the Lord speak distinctly

"Pick them up."

"Lord, they are going the opposite direction I'm going, I can't. Besides, I have this appointment with mom."

"Pick them up" he emphatically repeated.

I decided to "put out a fleece." If you don't know what I'm talking about I suggest you look up Judges 6:36-40. I said

"Okay God, if mom is not home, I'll come back and give them a ride."

I drove on to mom's fully confident she would be waiting just as she had all the times before. When I got to her house she was not only gone, but there was a note saying she and dad had gone to Arkansas for a visit with relatives.

"Okay, God I got the message."

I returned to get the couple. They knew who I was when I pulled over.

"Don't you just live down the road there? Is that all the further you are going to give us a ride?"

"No, come on and get in. I'll give you a ride at least to the intersection" (about 5 miles East). I shared with them how God had directed me to pick them up. They listened quietly to this strange man. By the time I got to the intersection God had me convinced I needed to take them all the way to Paris. They were headed to a factory there to apply for jobs. When we arrived I asked them if I could pray for them. I prayed that God would help them get jobs and direct their steps.

As I drove out of the parking lot I heard God say

"Go get gas." I looked at the gauge laying on empty and said

"Oh, thank you Lord." As I neared the gas station I heard him say

"Put in $5.00 worth."

I smiled and said "I got cha Lord; you are timing me perfect so I can pick up that couple on their way home." I moved about at a slow casual pace thinking I was walking in God's perfect timing. I returned to the car after paying the attendant and began heading back West on rt. 133. When I came up to the stop sign on route 1 I heard God say

"Turn South."

"But God" I argued, "they are gonna be waiting on me."

"Turn south" he again emphatically repeated.

"Okay." I began to think of who I knew in the South end of Paris. "Oh yeah, Betty is working at a restaurant down here. God probably wants me to give her some encouragement." Betty had just recently accepted Jesus at our property. I was ready to turn into the parking lot and again God spoke

"Keep going south." My faith was really being tested now. Rather sarcastically I said

"Where are we going? To Florida?" I knew my faith would not hold out much further with this voice I was hearing. I came upon a hitch-hiker and God said

"Pick him up." I was wondering just how far we were going to go with this trip. I stopped and picked him up.

After small talk he began to pour out his story to me. A few years ago he had a very successful veterinary service. His beloved wife had contracted cancer and he watched her slowly deteriorate from its insidious invasion of her body. He described how toward the end he could pick her up easily in his two hands she was so wasted away.

"Every animal that got that bad I would put under in my business, but I couldn't do that with my wife." "When she died I closed my doors, left my home and hit the road. I've wandered homeless and a vagabond ever since." I shared how God had directed me to him and I believed God wanted to help him get his life back together. I pulled over as both of us were now shedding tears. He went on to say "Last night I was wandering the streets of Paris kicking bottles and cans trying to find a few more drops of liquor. This song came to me." I listened as he sang the song "In times like these you need a Savior. In times like these you need an anchor. Be very sure, be very sure, your anchor holds and grips the solid rock." It was evident God was at work. I prayed with him and then suggested he go back home with me and get a hot bath, a hot meal, a good night's sleep in a warm bed and then head back home to his daughter. He agreed.

As we came back to the factory where I had let the two off earlier, guess what? Yep, they were standing and waiting on a ride. They got their desired jobs and thanked me for the prayers. All of us had a boost in our faith as we each shared the things God had done over the last several hours. When we got home I gave the old fellow all I had promised. He was happy to receive such attention, but he did not want to stay the night. "I want to get started back to my daughter's. Just take me to the next town and I'll head back to her." I had told him earlier that Oakland was a "dry" town and the nearest tavern was the next town West. I drove him there. When I pulled up to the door of the tavern he said

"What are you doing stopping here?"

I said "Let's quit playing games. You know this is where you want to go."

He got angry and said "You have no idea what it's like. Yes, I gotta have alcohol. It's a burning craving in me."

"You are right, I don't know what it's like, but let me tell you something. When you drink this time its not gonna be like any other time. You are gonna get very sick and when you do give me a call."

I left him my phone number and headed home. Sure enough about an hour or two later my phone rang and he said "Would you come and get me? I'm so sick."

"I'll be right there."

When I arrived he was nowhere to be found. I asked the folks inside if they knew where he was and they said they saw someone give him a ride. I prayed for him and let him go. I trust him to God. I know good seed was planted and I knew he knew he had been loved and pursued in an unusual way. I trust God continues to help him get his life back together. It was quite a day indeed.

A COUPLE MORE GOOD
EXPERIENCES

Another interesting incident happened during those 30 years. I made a trip to Key West trying to run from myself. I had stopped at a fast food place and picked up a lunch which I took to one of the many beaches in the keys and was sitting there enjoying the scenery and eating my meal. A car pulled up and two beautiful gals in bikinis got out and walked to a nearby table. I could not help but notice the beauty and like most men felt lust tugging at my sleeve. I pondered how pitiful and shameful that we can't admire beauty without the ugliness of lust. "Such beauty deserves a compliment" I thought, but I was not about to go give it. Then I felt the "nudge" from God to go tell them so. I fought the urge off as just part of the flesh, but the "nudge" continued. Finally, I gave in to what I hoped was a "call" from God and approached them. I don't remember exactly what I said but something along the lines "I was just admiring your beauty and thought it a shame that we live in a world where one cannot express appreciation without it being turned into something ugly." They expressed their appreciation rather questioningly, but it opened the door for deeper conversation. As we talked about God's ability to create things beautiful, the one girl took a real interest in conversation about God, while the other wandered off to play in the surf. She told me how she was Jewish and had just returned from Israel. She had gone over there in hopes of finding something meaningful in her racial heritage.

She said "it doesn't mean a thing to me to be Jewish." She even sounded rather bitter about it.

"Oh no" I responded, "You shouldn't feel that way." I began to explain to her how she ought to be proud of her heritage. I took her back to Abraham, the father of all Israel and told how he was a friend of God and had a very deep and personal relationship with God because he trusted Him. I must have spent 45 minutes to an hour telling the story of the Jews through the centuries and how God wanted to show the whole world how good and kind He is. I could tell she was eating it up. It's like she had never heard the good side of being a descendant of Israel.

"Besides all that" I began to conclude, "you should be looking for the promised Messiah who will come and bring perfect peace and love to earth." I shared the Scriptures that pointed forward to a coming Messiah. The Spirit of God was bringing Scripture after Scripture to my mind and leading her along as she seemed to feed on every word I shared. Finally, I brought it to a conclusion that startled her. I said "actually this Messiah has come and brought His kingdom to earth. He has brought perfect love and peace to all who accept Him." As I ended with the words "And His name is Jesus of Nazareth" I saw every human emotion flash through her eyes and I distinctly heard the voice of God loud and clear "Get up and leave her with that." I obeyed. She sat there speechless as I walked away, got in my car and drove off. I believe the Spirit of God stayed with her and began a process that eventually led her to embrace Jesus Christ as her Messiah and Savior. I believe I will see her in heaven where she will finally again meet up with the strange man that met her on the beach and introduced her to the Answer of her search. God was using me in spite of the captivity I was wrestling with.

I want to mention one more good experience during those captive, insane years. In spite of my debauchery God used me to save souls. My daughter Teresa, her husband Carl along with their three boys had moved to Colorado. I decided to spend some time with them. When I was about ready to return to Illinois the fellow Carl was working for came and asked me to build a cabin way back in the mountains that he did not have time to do. I always wanted to build a cabin in the mountains so I said "sign him up."

The contractor gave me a helper named John who helped me the 6 weeks it took to build the cabin. John had a drinking problem as well as other issues in his troubled life. Every day I talked to him about the goodness of God who made all that beautiful creation surrounding us. It made John very nervous at first, but the Spirit worked on him. When I returned to Illinois he called me up one day.

"Bob, I want to come out and work for you. You don't even have to pay me. Whatever it is that you have, I think I want it."

We spent that first evening in my home visiting in our living room. I asked him:

"John if you died tonight do you know for sure you would go to heaven?"

"I know for sure that I would go to hell" he replied.

"If you'll hang around and listen to what I share with you that will change."

Over the next 6 weeks or so John changed. By the time he left he knew for sure that he was going to heaven. He accepted Jesus as his Savior. He was born again, born from above, born from the Word of God. His name was written in the Lamb's book of life. He attended a Sunday School class I was teaching which had grown from 3 or 4 to about 30 or 40. I had asked all of them the same question: "Do you know for sure that you are going to heaven?" None were sure, at least they weren't sure until we had done a study on the book of Romans and other Scriptures and then they were sure. If you doubt that a person can know for sure that he/she is going to heaven you should check out I John 5:13 "These things I have written unto you who believe in the name of the Son of God, that you may KNOW that you have eternal life." A good study of what is "written" can bring you to a position of full assurance. God wants his children to know they are His and they are safe in His kingdom.

Today John not only has a strong Christian family but one of his sons has become a minister of the Word of God. God is able to use even his wayfaring children to spread the Gospel. He used me when I was deep in sin. He can use a donkey, rooster, rock or as Don Francisco sings "the dog next door." Nothing is too hard for our God.

PART FIVE

Deliverance and Restoration

IT'S DONE, OVER,
THROUGH, ENDED

God only knows the hell I went through those 30 years. When I look back I hardly know that man. He was so lost within himself. He had lost touch with reality. He was blind. He could not save himself. He was like a walking dead man. Perhaps that's what it took. He needed to have something within him die . . . and it did.

It's a miracle hard to describe. Here you are living for 30 long years in bondage to sin and one day it suddenly ends. How does that happen? My partner and I came to a realization one day that it could not go on. We knew we were hurting too many people. I guess it was like the prodigal son who finally got so low that "he came to his senses." Something like that happened to us. We agreed that the sin had to end . . . but at the same time we recognized that not everything in our relationship was sin. We were friends; we loved one another . . . that was not wrong. Was it possible to have such a drastic shift made in our relationship? It happened.

Again, I can't explain that, I can only testify that from that day the lust, adultery and sexual sin came to a complete and total end and God replaced it with a pure friendship and love. Only God can do that. As He had promised 30 years before "I will bring you through" and He did. But He did more than deliver us from sin; He went on to transform us to be able to share a beautiful friendship. I don't know which the greater miracle was, but I know now that "nothing is too hard for the Lord." He can do the impossible.

A Door Opens Immediately

Any ministry in my life had pretty well ground to a halt over those years. But almost the day the transformation took place I got a call to preach in a nearby church. I was uncertain about taking the position. Although they begged me to come I wasn't sure what their reaction would be if and when they discovered my past. Without giving them the details I did tell them I had a sordid past, but there were three things they needed to know about it. 1. It's all forgiven. 2. It is forgotten (Heb. 10:17 "Their sins and their lawless deeds I will remember no more.") 3. It is forsaken. Forgiven, Forgotten and Forsaken! My sin is gone. I agreed to preach for them on a temporary basis. "Let us spend a few months together before we make it permanent. If either of us is not happy with the arrangements then we can peacefully call it quits." They agreed.

After about 7 months we made it "permanent." I became their full-time pastor. I did stress one point. If at some time in the future you don't want me as your pastor, let us sit down and respectfully and honorably discuss it. I had been "thrown out" of several churches in the past and I didn't want that to happen again. (Of the 16 churches I've been deeply involved in half of them treated me with dishonor and disrespect and half of them honored me. That's probably a better record than the prophets and apostles had).

Guess what! Two years later I was "kicked out." There was no sit down and have a respectable discussion. There was no honor involved. Someone had made the rounds and let everyone in the church know about my past and turned their hearts against me. I was rail-roaded out.

I won't go into the details, but believe me, God's people can do some very under-handed and even illegal things to get done what they want done. Sad story. I was learning that even though YOU may be through with your sin, your enemy isn't. He will use your past against you in every way he can. I would learn that all the more a few years later.

RESOLVING, REACTIONS AND OVER-REACTIONS

It was seven years ago in 2005 that the Lord ended the 30 years of adultery. Although it has never even come close to ever returning, the enemy has screamed at me over and over that I'm no different than I ever was. Sometimes he uses people to make those screams; more often he uses my own heart. I have had to remind myself over and over the teaching of John in I John 3:20 "For if our heart condemns us, God is greater than our heart, and knows all things." I don't know all things. People don't know all things. Satan doesn't know all things. Only God does, and He knows that I'm not the man I was. I've been redeemed. I've been set free. It's what God thinks of me that's really important, not what other people or the devil thinks of me. I have to fight to keep that clear in my thinking.

My family stood by me in the battle within that little church. Although I had indeed hurt them deeply, they believed in me. They believed I was a changed man. We still had our problems, but we were working through them. We were all getting better.

I had written letters, made phone calls, and had personal talks with everyone in my family. I had made apologies, confessions and tried every way I could to make things right. How do you resolve 30 years of pain? How do you make up for 30 years of failure? You can only say "I'm sorry" so many times and in so many ways. I tried every way I could think of. We were working our way through it. It was definitely being resolved at God's pace and in accordance with His plan.

During this "resolving" time I asked God to help me see and feel the pain I had brought to so many people. He answered me. For 6 weeks I took them one by one into my heart and He let me feel their pain. I cried a river of tears over those weeks. I never felt such love and yet such remorse and sorrow. It was a good sorrow. It produced a very deep repentance and resolving. At the end of those weeks He said . . . "Enough. You have done all you can do. You have felt their pain. You have apologized. You have done all you can do to resolve it. Now, let it go. Let it go and go on with your life." I began to do just that.

Some of my family had started going to a rather large church in a nearby town. They convinced me to join them. It was good. The fellowship, teaching and worship were a good blend of worship and learning. We were growing together. Two in the family felt the need to work through some of the pain of the past. Although I believe God was gently working us all through that pain, they felt the need of getting professional counseling in the big church. They began going to the church counselor.

When she found out what my past was I believe she over-reacted. Her remark was "there is an elephant in the room that has been ignored too long." To me she "made an elephant out of a flea," or "a mountain out of a mole-hill." She brought feelings back to the two girls that had been on the mend. She opened old sores that were healing and brought forth fresh blood. She supported them in setting boundaries on me and my former lover. She did not believe it was possible for me and her to be the friends that we had become. A certain law seem to develop that began to spread to the girls and through the church. Although that law, to my knowledge never has been written it would read something like this "THOU SHALT NOT BE FRIEND TODAY WITH ANYONE WITH WHOM YOU HAVE LIVED IN SIN IN THE PAST."

The two girls adopted that law and tried their best to force it upon us. We were not allowed to show up at either of their houses together. It didn't stop there. They took this concern to the pastor and convinced him they were in the right.

During this time, in 2009 I came down with cancer and ended up for surgery in the hospital. Two significant things happened to me while in the hospital. The first came about two days after my surgery when they finally brought me some solid food. There was one bite of mashed potatoes left on my plate. I looked down and there in that wad of potatoes was a perfect cross. Well, that in itself might not be very significant, but what makes it significant was what happened when I saw that cross. I was listening to an IPod I had borrowed and the song "It is well" was playing in my ear. "My sin, oh the bliss of this glorious thought, my sin not in part but the whole, is nailed to the cross and I bear it no more, praise the Lord, praise the Lord oh my soul." When the word "cross" came into my ear, that is the moment I spied the cross on the potatoes. It gave me goose bumps. I understand that God was driving a point home. I need to be reminded over and over that my sin is indeed FORGIVEN, FORGOTTEN AND FORSAKEN. When we are down, depressed, worn out and weary we are more subject to the temptation and lies the devil throws at us. I needed that emphatic reminder that "It is well with my soul" because the heat was about to be turned up . . . . I'll get to that a little later.

The second significant thing that happened in that hospital was the miracle God did in my marriage. He began to put me and my wife back together. For the first time in 20 years she reached out to me in that bed and gave me a hug. When you face cancer and the prospect that you are indeed terminal and that it could be sooner rather than later it begins to change a lot of things in your life. You quit resisting God for one thing. You open up more and more to whatever He wants to do in your life. Piece by piece He began to put me and Peggy back together after many years of separation. Neither of us believed that we would ever get back together. All hope of that was gone. I had wandered too far. I knew of no way to fix the marriage and had no intention of even trying. It was strictly a work of God that we began to heal.

As God continued to process that healing we decided we wanted to give testimony at church about what God was doing in healing our marriage. We had moved from the big church in town to a small "sister" or "mother" church in the country. It was arranged for us to share the Sunday just before our 57th wedding anniversary. We were pretty excited about sharing the good things God was doing.

The Saturday night before the Sunday morning when we were to share I got a telephone call from the pastor of the big church. He informed me we were not allowed to give our testimony. I was a bit mystified and asked him why. He said "Because of your ongoing relationship with your former lover" or something along those lines. I knew then that the girls and the counselor had "got through to him." The law was being enforced "THOU SHALT NOT HAVE A FRIENDSHIP TODAY WITH ANYONE WITH WHOM YOU HAD A SINFUL RELATIONSHIP WITH IN THE PAST." A restraint was put upon me from sharing in the pulpit of either the big or the smaller church.

My Defense to My Accusers

The pastor of the big church said this was the decision of the elders. I asked to meet with those elders and give my defense. A few days later Peggy and I met with the pastor and the elders and I presented my defense. In brief this is what I shared:

"God has done five great miracles in my life. The first miracle was my salvation which took place in 1960 in my father-in-law's woods. After two weeks of intense and fervent prayer I surrendered my destiny to the hands of God and committed myself to Jesus Christ and His kingdom. In a deep and impressionable experience God let me know "NOW YOU ARE ACCEPTED." From that day on I can echo the words of Paul in II Tim.1:12 "I know whom I have believed and am persuaded that He is able to keep what I have committed to Him until that Day." I placed my salvation into His hands and He took care of it and has never put it back into my hands.

The second great miracle that stands out in my life was how God preserved me through those 30 years of adultery. By all rights I should be dead or dying from STD or at the hands of some jealous husband. I should have lost my faith, my health, and my sanity and ended up in the grave or the penitentiary. It's a miracle I was preserved and survived. God was faithful to do exactly as He promised: "I will take you through this Red Sea, this fiery furnace, this lion's den." And He did.

The third great miracle He did was delivering me from those 30 years. By the power of His love and His Spirit He set me free. He ended it. I was changed. I'm not the same man I was. "I became a new creature, old things have passed away; behold, all things have become new." II Cor.5:17.

The fourth great miracle was one of transformation. He took what was formerly a sinful adulterous relationship and transformed it into one of true love and friendship. Only God could do that. Many believe He cannot do that, but nothing is impossible with God. He did the impossible. He is like that. I went on to explain how the story of David and Bathsheba was similar to the story of me and my former lover. David, like me had caved in to his lust when he saw naked Bathsheba bathing. He took this married women, had sex with her, got her pregnant and then used cunning and deceit to kill her husband and take her to be his wife. They deserved to die for their sin, but God sent the prophet Nathan to bring him to repentance. After the death of the baby, after the repentance and resolving of the past sin God forgave them and not only allowed them to become good friends, He let them marry, blessed their marriage, blessed their next child, gave him a name and made that child the next king of Israel. That was a miracle transformation that He still does in the lives of those who trust Him and that's what He did for us. Their past was forgiven, forgotten and forsaken and so was ours.

The fifth great miracle I testified to that group was how He put our marriage back together. We had lost all hope. Neither of us believed it could ever be done. We never expected it to be done. It was a complete surprise. Again, nothing is too hard for the Lord and in all five miracles He showed His divine abilities. We rejoiced in all that He had done."

The pastor and elders did not share our joy. There were no "hallelujahs" in that room that night (except our own). They did not believe the fourth miracle was complete. Again, they were persuaded "That you cannot be a good friend with anyone today with whom you have sinned in the past." They refused to believe that God could do as much for us as He had done for David and Bathsheba. To reject any one of those five miracles is to reject them all. God did each of them with the same power, love, grace, mercy and forgiveness. They stand as a unit.

Not only did the elders sustain the restraint by not allowing us to testify in church, they took it before the whole church and give them to know that we were being disciplined by the church. We were not informed of this public meeting that discussed our supposed sin and rebellion. We do not know today what specific charges were brought against us and shared with those who attended that meeting. A request for a copy of the DVD or tape that was made of that meeting was denied us. We do not know today what they consider to be our great evil even though I have asked time and again to have it explained to me.

It is commonly believed in psychology and counseling that one cannot continue a friendship with someone with whom you have had an affair. I suppose that could be true in most cases, but I'm also sure that God can make exceptions to that (as He did with David and Bathsheba). A great emphasis is put upon the value of counseling, psychology and recovery in our churches today. I would never say that those elements are not important, but I think way too often the work of the Holy Spirit and the power of the Gospel is under-valued in changing the behavior of fallen human beings. I'm convinced that in many cases a sincere surrender and repentance at an old-fashioned altar for 15-20 minutes could do more to correct sinful behavior than 6 months of sitting in a professional counselor's office. No human, whether it's a counselor, pastor, pope, priest or surgeon can match the power of the Holy Spirit when it comes to changing lives. It seems we have forgotten that "nothing is impossible with God." Paul made it clear in many Scriptures that his intent was to share the gospel because he believed it was the only real answer for putting people right with God. "For I am not ashamed of the gospel of Christ, for it is the power of God to salvation for everyone who believes, for the Jew first and also for the Greek." (Rom. 1:16). He wrote to the Corinthians and emphatically said "I determined not to know anything among you except Jesus Christ and Him crucified." I Cor. 2:2. Churches today seem to have lost confidence in the power of the gospel and the life changing ministry of the Holy Spirit and often resort to human psychology, philosophy and intellectualism to remedy human behavior.

MY FIVE GUIDING PRINCIPLES

I've had to forgive these people. I've tried to explain to them how I know that what I'm doing is the right thing. I have shared five principles I follow to determine right and good behavior.

The first principle is to ask "what would Jesus do?" We can answer that by looking to see what He did. How did He treat sinful women? Look at how He treated the woman caught in adultery. Did He withdraw from her? Did he join the crowd in finding fault and accusing her? No! He chased off her accusers and showed her he accepted her the way she was. When she realized He was not going to "rake her across the coals" or bring charges against her or reject her . . . then . . . and only then . . . he told her "Go and sin no more." We want to turn that around. We try to get people to stop their sin before we accept them. We don't drop our stones until we "lay down the law." We are quicker to crucify than to edify. As has been often said "the church is the only army that shoots its wounded." We want to control people rather than wash their feet. That is not Jesus' way. Look at Him with the woman at the well, with Mary Magdalene and the woman caught in the act of adultery. We need to learn to treat sinners the way He did. He is my example when it comes to how I treat my former lover.

The second principle I seek to follow is the principle of agape love. Read I Cor. 13 to see how that love operates. "Love suffers long and is kind; love does not envy; does not behave rudely, does not seek its own, is not provoked, thinks no evil; does not rejoice in iniquity, but rejoices in the truth; bears all things, believes all things, hopes all things, endures all things. Love never fails." I'm always amazed how quickly humans can turn on one another. How they can lose their faith in one another. So many have a love that grows cold easily and cannot endure when the going gets rough. Agape love does not quit. It keeps on believing in people.

The third principle I follow for guidance and direction is to heed the Word of God. I'm convinced there is an answer to every problem in the Word of God. Paul wrote to Timothy in II Tim. 3:16, 17 "All Scripture is given by inspiration of God, and is profitable for doctrine, for reproof, for correction, for instruction in righteousness, that the man of God may be complete, thoroughly equipped for every good work." As I proved earlier, God can transform sinful relationships into acceptable and blessed ones. It's in the Word. It's in the Bible. It's in the story of David and Bathsheba. Read it in II Samuel 11 & 12. I believe and follow it.

The fourth principle I follow is the guidance and instruction of God's Holy Spirit. It would take a book to tell all the ways God's Spirit has spoke to me and directed me over my 77 years. Time and again He has given me those strong impressions "this is the way, walk ye in it." Take a long look at Heb. 8:8-11 (It's repeated in chapter 10). "Behold the days are coming, says the Lord, when I will make a new covenant with the house of Israel and with the house of Judah . . . not according to the covenant that I made with their fathers in the day when I took them by the hand to lead them out of the land of Egypt; because they did not continue in my covenant, and I disregarded them, says the Lord. For this is the covenant that I will make with the house of Israel after those days, says the Lord, I WILL PUT MY LAWS IN THEIR MIND AND WRITE THEM ON THEIR HEARTS; and I will be their God, and they shall be My people. None of them shall teach his neighbor, and none his brother, saying, Know the Lord, for all shall know me, from the least of them to the greatest of them." Do you get that message? We have the promise of the indwelling of the Holy Spirit to tell us what to do and what not to do. Isn't that wonderful? Don't you appreciate that? You don't have to run around telling everyone what to do. That's the Holy Spirit's job. He does it well. You just need to tell people "Do what God tells you to do." We need teachers to teach us that. That's what pastors and teachers and elders are supposed to do . . . tell people to obey God . . . obey the Spirit . . . do what He is writing on your heart and mind. That is great news. When people don't believe the Spirit is doing that, they try to do it themselves. That's where we get into lots of trouble. Too many folks are out there trying to do the Holy Spirit's work. So few seem to believe that He is capable of doing His own job.

I like to remind folks of the young prophet who was sent from Judea down to Samaria to cry out against the substitute altar that had been built there. God told him "Don't stop and visit. Don't eat or drink anywhere down there. Just go do your job and come straight back." You can read the story in I Kings chapter 13. Well, he went down and did the job. When he cried against the altar it crumbled and the ashes fell out. King Jeroboam was there worshipping and when he saw and heard what the prophet did he stretched out his hand and pointed to the prophet and cried "Seize that man." Immediately his out-stretched hand turned to leprosy. Then he begged the prophet to pray for him. The prophet did and the king was healed. This prophet was anointed. He was anointed and protected because he was doing what God told him to do even though the king was against him. The young prophet started home as God had told him to do. He did stop to rest under a shade tree and the sons of an old prophet caught up with him. They said "Our dad says the Lord has told him to tell you to come and have a meal with us." The young prophet said "I can't do that, God has told me not to." "Well, yes," they said, but our dad is a grand poo-bah. He has a doctorate in theology. He is a certified counselor. He has pastored many churches. Why he has even been the president of a Bible college. He says you must come because God has told him you are supposed to." What would you have done? Or what do you do? Do you follow your pastor? Do you follow your counselor? Who is your teacher? Who is your leader? Who is your God? The young prophet went home and ate with them. In the middle of the meal the old prophet finally spoke the truth . . . "You will not make it back home. You have disobeyed the Lord in coming to eat with us." (What a nice guy huh?) Sure enough a lion killed him on the way home. What's the lesson? DO WHAT GOD TELLS YOU TO DO NO MATTER WHO OR WHAT COMES UP TO THE CONTRARY. That's what I'm doing. I refuse to let some pastor, group of elders, a professional counselor, pope, priest or politician over-rule my

God. I hope you do the same. You do what God tells you to do even if it's in complete disagreement with me or anyone else. I believe the folks in that church are doing what they sincerely believe is right. I believe their ideas are right for them, but not for me.

The fifth and last principle I live by is to listen to the wise, compassionate and experienced advice of folks who I know truly love me. It's the folks that I know who are willing to wash my feet that I listen to. It's not those who are seeking to control my life and lay their man-made laws on me. Oh, I will respect their right to believe what they believe, but I do not respect their efforts to bring me under the laws written on their hearts. Romans 14 makes it clear that we will not always see eye to eye on everything. We are to respect one another, but not judge or set one another at naught. Be careful with this principle. Not everyone is being led by the Spirit. Many have their own agenda . . . their own rules . . . and they love to enforce them on other people. The church today is full of self-righteous critics and judges. Don't let them put you under their spell. Paul wrote many of his writings warning of false apostles, false teachers and false prophets. They are out there. Thank God when He surrounds you with folks who help you kindly, patiently, gently find the way. I praise God for all such that He has placed in my life. I value them and honor them highly. They have been great help to me in many tough times.

DEALING WITH DIFFERENCES

I don't want to be misunderstood. I'm a member of the fallen race. I'm a sinner. I "sin and fall short of the glory of God." Rom. 3:23. I understand Isa. 53:6 "All we like sheep have gone astray, we have turned every one to his own way." I agree with John "If we say we have not sinned, we make Him a liar, and His word is not in us." I John 1:10. I pray like the publican "Lord have mercy on me a sinner." But I confess every known sin in my life. I ask God daily to open my eyes to anything I'm blind to. I trust Him to help me day by day. My conscience is clear, but only God knows everything and He will be the final judge of all of us. I don't sit in judgment on anyone else. I forgive those who wrong me. How can I not forgive people of lesser sin when I have committed greater and received His forgiveness and grace. I try to pass on the mercy, grace, love and forgiveness that I have received. I try to live by Eph. 4:32 "Be kind to one another, tenderhearted, forgiving one another, even as God in Christ forgave you." But people and churches make up rules that I cannot keep up with. Here are a few I've run into over the years:

. . . . You shall not bring drums into the church.
. . . . You shall only have communion with one cup.
. . . . You shall baptize only in running water.
. . . . You must not speak in tongues in our church.
. . . . You must speak in tongues to be part of our church.
. . . . You must use only the King James Version Bible in our church.
. . . . If you are a woman you must pray only with a covering on your head.
. . . . You cannot take communion if you've not been baptized.

. . . . You must be baptized and that only by immersion.

. . . . Men must not let their hair grow long.

. . . . Women must not cut their hair short.

. . . . You must meet on Sundays.

. . . . You must meet on Saturdays.

. . . . And of course one of the latest: "you must not be friends with anyone today with whom you have committed sin in the past." This list could go on and on. Every church has their own by-laws, rules and regulations. Some have them written out and others are just a common understanding among the "loyal" members. Every individual has boundaries. Every family has an understanding of what is acceptable and what is not. We have a right to draw our lines and enforce our boundaries. However, we need to be careful about forcing our boundaries on other people. Romans 14 makes it clear that there will always be differences among God's people. We need to respect those differences. We need to honor one another. Often we need to agree to disagree. We should not flaunt our freedoms. We are free to have a beer or glass of wine but we ought not to flaunt that freedom before those who are wrestling with alcoholism. We need to "do unto others as we would have them do unto us." We need to honor and respect others in the same way we want them to honor and respect us.

Something needs to be said about "offending others" or "causing them to stumble." Just because someone doesn't like what you are doing does not mean he will be "offended" or "stumble." People are pretty strong in their own beliefs. Someone drinking a beer in front of me is not going to cause me to have one . . . even if he tries to coax me into it. I'm not offended nor do I stumble by his freedom. I respect his freedom. He should also respect my freedom to abstain. The trouble comes when we try to force our own boundaries on other people. If a church has boundaries too restrictive for you to live under, then leave that church. There is no cause to try to "straighten them out." Nor should they follow you around and put their restrictions on you (as the latest church in my life has tried to do.) A lot can be said in defense of the old adage "live and let live." It's certainly better than trying to force people to "live as we live." I've often said many churches will sing "Just as I am" on

Sunday morning to get you to come as you are and accept Jesus into your life so He can make any necessary changes. But by Wednesday night, or the next Sunday, or sometime soon in the future they begin to pressure you to "come and be like us." "Just as I am" goes out the door all too quickly. Churches today are in great need of learning grace and mercy and how to bathe one another in the blood of Jesus and the benefits of the gospel. We don't change people, God does. We need to trust people to the Holy Spirit. We need a revival of real faith and trust in God. There is way too much human ingenuity and psychology being used to alter human behavior and not enough preaching of the Gospel and calls to repentance. We need more new births and new creations rather than psychological pressures to change. Let's get back to believing in God who specializing in doing the impossible. How can we get any better than that?

THE GRAND FINALE

A Special Dream and its Meaning

Writing the last chapter of a book of one's life is a challenge as life normally continues to roll on. I had been pondering how to wrap this up and then it came. About midnight and for the next hour on November 22, 2012, Thanksgiving Day it came to me. Quite an appropriate time since Thanksgiving is my favorite holiday. I grabbed a yellow note pad and began to hand write it all down at 1:00 in the morning. Everything you have read that has happened in my life, from my mother's attempted abortion to the recent rejection, accusation and unfair restrictions from an area church have all brought me to this finale . . . to my death. A death that is summed up in several Scriptures: Gal. 2:20 **"I am crucified with Christ it is no longer I who live**, but Christ lives in me and the life which I now live in the flesh I live by faith in the Son of God, who loved me and gave Himself for me." Also in Phil 3:10 "That I may know Him and the power of His resurrection, and the fellowship of His sufferings, being **conformed to His death**, if, by any means, I may attain to the resurrection from the dead." John the Baptist explained what I'm trying to say when he said in John 3:30 "He must increase (Jesus) and I must decrease." We are called to die with Christ, to lose our life, to take up our cross and follow Him. Our life is meant to be about Jesus, who He is and what He has done. It takes a death to self to see and experience His life manifest and magnified in us.

Forty years ago this came to me in a dream from God. I dreamed I was in my living room with several of the Jesus People or Christ Kids of that era. Suddenly we heard the song How Great Thou Art being sung by a choir. It grew louder and louder. The kids asked me "What is that?" Instantly I knew and told them "It's a great choir of angels. Jesus is coming." I turned and ran up the stairs and into my study. I fell on my knees at the window that faced the East. I could see the Eastern sky starting to light up. It was getting brighter and brighter and I knew that Jesus was going to come up over the horizon at any second. I was thrilled, excited and full of anticipation. But, then He stopped just below the horizon. "No" I thought as I felt the pause of his coming. Then my attention was drawn to something high in the sky off to my right. I turned my head and looked up and saw two crosses. They were a brilliant shining white. I supposed the light to be what is described as the Shekinah glory of God. One of the crosses was much larger with the little one off to the left. I was mystified at them and pondered what they could mean. Then my attention was drawn to my hands on the window sill. I looked down and my hands and fingers were glowing with the same bright light. When I awoke I entered a day that had more strange things happen than any day I've ever lived. I won't go into all those things, but mostly they seem to indicate that Jesus' return is soon.

I have pondered over the years what that dream meant. Now I believe I understand. One thing for sure: Jesus is coming and He is coming soon, very likely in my life-time or immediately after my death. I do believe the two crosses represent His death and mine. I think my death is the one Paul described in Gal. 2:20 and the other Scriptures I've quoted above. We are called to die to our own ways. Everything that has happened in my life was meant to kill me. All the good, the bad, the ugly has been with the intention of bringing me to an end of myself and to form Christ within me. As John the Baptist said "He must increase and I must decrease."

Over the years many people have hurt me in many different ways. These hurts have helped expedite this death to self. Please know that I love and forgive you, just as Joseph loved and forgave his brothers who had treated him so cruelly. Further, like Joseph, I understand all these things happened under the hand of God and were meant for good, not evil. (Genesis 50:20) All these things as Paul says in Romans 8:28, 29 work out for good, and he explains exactly what that "good" is. "And we know that all things work together for good to those who love God, to those who are the called according to His purpose. For whom He foreknew, He also predestined to BE CONFORMED TO THE IMAGE OF HIS SON." We don't become "conformed to the image of His Son" without dying and getting out of the way. All of life's circumstances, situations and relationships are leading us in that precious direction.

The hands that have written this book have been anointed with that Shikinah glory. They are anointed with my death and His life, love and light. It has all come down to being a blessing for you dear reader. You have been blessed by reading the story of Jesus in my life. I have prayed for months for every one of you. Jesus has walked In My Steps for 77 years and has now reached out through my anointed hands to share the story . . . His Story . . . through my hands. Some of you will be healed of physical sickness and infirmity by this story. Some of you will be delivered from alcohol, nicotine and other drugs. Some of you will be delivered from homosexuality, adultery and other sexual sins. Some of you will be strengthened to resist the temptation to abort your tiny baby. Some of you will receive that light, life and love of Jesus that will renew your mind and spirit and you will know a real revival, restoration and transformation in your heart and mind.

But far more important than any of those miracles, some of you will receive Jesus as the Savior of your soul. You will be born again, redeemed, saved. Your name will be written in the Lamb's book of life and you will receive His precious promised Holy Spirit. You will cause the angels to rejoice over your repentance and consequent salvation. I rejoice with you now, even as I am writing this. It is sure to come.

God taught me several years ago to begin praying as commanded in I Tim. 2:1-6 "I exhort first of all that supplication, prayers, intercessions, and giving of thanks be made FOR ALL MEN, for kings and all who are in authority, that we may lead a quiet and peaceable life in all godliness and reverence. For this is good and acceptable in the sight of God our Savior, who desires all men to be saved and to come to the knowledge of the truth. For there is one God and one Mediator between God and man, the Man Christ Jesus, who have Himself a ransom for all, to be testified in due time." I have learned that when I pray for the 7 billion people on earth the Holy Spirit joins me and prays along with me "with groaning that cannot be uttered." Romans 8:26, 27. As I pray for each and every nation he prays for every individual by name and by need. He not only knows every human being by name, but He knows how many hairs are on their body, He bottles up their every tear, He knows them intimately as described in Psalms 139. James puts the capstone on this kind of praying when he says "The effectual fervent prayer of a righteous man AVAILS MUCH." James 5:16. "Avails much" means it accomplishes a lot, or makes a big difference. This is a practice every believer ought to engage in. God says in Jeremiah 33:3 "Call unto Me, and I will answer you, and show you great and mighty things, which you do not know." You have no idea how great an effect you are having on the world around you. Jesus said "you are the light of the world and the salt of the earth." The very life of Jesus is in His people and it flows out to the world around them. Evil is restrained; good is encouraged by our very presence. The world will see what our effect is once we are taken out and the spirit of anti-Christ begins to prevail. We need to understand how great that "power that works in us."

ALL FOR ONE PURPOSE
IN MY STEPS

Let us yoke with Him, die with Him, and abide in Him. He is all in all, the First and the Last, the Alpha and Omega, the Beginning and the End. He is coming and His reward is with Him. Let us be like Paul's hanky that healed people, or like Elisha's bones that brought a man back to life (II Kings 13:21). Or like Peter's shadow, or the hem of Jesus' garment, or a mere crumb from the Master's table or a single word from the Commander-in-Chief's tongue. Receive this book with the impact God wants it to have on your life. Dozens, hundreds, thousands will be blessed. God is blessing you. Receive it.

A dear brother who was dismissed from Bible College along with me way back in 1957 has a few good words along these lines:

"There are countless examples of godly men and women who continue to exert lively influence, even though they have departed the realm we now occupy. Moses, the Prophets, John the Baptist, and the Apostles, are cases in point. Throughout history, there has been a trail of holy personalities who still have power, so to speak, in their "bones." It only takes a touch of their literary remains to confirm this to be the case. How often I have been refreshed by the expressions of those who have completed their course, but left behind something tangible that can be touched. It appears to me that it is a noble intention to leave something of profit behind—some "bones," so to speak, that can have a godly affect upon those who touch them. Your words, deeds, and writings can potentially have that kind of power. Believe it!"—Given O. Blakely

CONCLUSION

It has been my intent to expose to you the greatest adventure there is in life; what it means to have Jesus Christ walk in your feet, live in your heart, think with your mind, and work with your hands; to live His life in you. That is my simple but most challenging goal. I think of the voyage of the star ship Enterprise "to boldly go where no man has ever gone before." That's my goal in the Spirit "to go where no man has ever gone before." I remind myself continually of God's great promises. Eph. 3:20 "Now to Him who is able to do exceedingly abundantly above all that we ask or think, according to the power that works in us, to Him be glory in the church by Christ Jesus to all generations, forever and ever. Amen." Do you hear that? God offers us more than we have ever asked or imagined. Do you feel that hunger and thirst for more of God? He has great adventures for His people, but most of us are content to make mud pies in the pool behind the house rather than go to an island paradise or mountain top with Him.

We serve a great big infinite, sovereign adventuresome God. He constantly calls us to higher, richer, much more abundant and fruitful life. Most of humanity chooses to follow the "course of this world" Eph. 2:1-3. We go after what we want "All we like sheep have gone astray; we have turned, every one, to his own way; and the Lord has laid on Him the iniquity of us all" Isa. 53:6. We do not know or follow His ways and thoughts "For my thoughts are not your thoughts, nor are your ways My ways says the Lord. For as the heavens are higher than the earth, so are My ways higher than your ways, and My thoughts than your thoughts." We put such great limits on our experience by following "our own way" or the way of the flesh, or the way of the man-made, humanly organized church, or the way of intellectualism, philosophy and pop psychology. We are constantly being offered the vibrant, powerful life of the Vine. He wants to flow into us branches and produce rich, ripe effectual and abundant fruit John 15:1-8. He wants us to yoke up with Him and be partner in building His kingdom and raising His bountiful fields for harvest Matt. 11:28-30. He is a loving Shepherd, a kind patient Master and wants to direct our steps to rich green pastures and much higher purposes. Why are we content to follow our own foolish, fruitless, selfish, personal desires? Why do we think "it's my life and I'll live it the way I want?" Don't we understand "or do you not know that your body is the temple of the Holy Spirit who is in you, whom you have from God and you are not your own? For you were bought at a price; therefore glorify God in your body and in your spirit, which are God's" I Cor. 6:19, 20. How dare we withhold what is rightfully His?

It's your choice what you do with your life. "And if it seems evil to you to serve the Lord, choose for yourselves this day whom you will serve. But as for me and my house, we will serve the Lord" Joshua 24:15. Too much of my 77 years I chose to serve my own desires; I lived for my own interests. I am determined to "finish strong." I want to live the rest of my life fully submitted to Jesus Christ and let Him live His life in me. I want Him to walk "In My Steps" work with my hands, love through my heart, and speak through my mouth, Master my life to His praise and glory. I desperately want that abundant "much more" life. I am sick of trying to please men and myself. I want to live in His pleasure, yoked to Him, abiding in Him, obeying and following Him wherever he leads.

I believe all that has happened in my life and yours has brought us to this. God wants to give us more than we can ever imagine "eye has not seen, nor ear heard, nor have entered into the heart of man the things which God has prepared for those who love Him" I Cor. 2:9. Are you content to live only with the best man has to offer? Or do you, like me, hunger and thirst for more and more of Jesus Christ? Are you tired of being "conformed to this world" (even the "church world?") Do you long to be "transformed by the renewing of your mind, that you may prove what is that good and acceptable and perfect will of God?" Romans 12:1, 2.

We are breathing the air of the last days. The clock is ticking. Jesus is soon to return. The enemy has pulled out all the stops and is violently destroying everyone he can. "For the devil has come down to you, having great wrath, because he knows that he has a short time" Rev. 12:12. Jesus warned "The thief does not come except to steal, and to kill, and to destroy. I have come that they may have life, and that they may have it more abundantly" John 10:10. Two great powers are after your life. To choose to serve yourself is to choose to follow the evil power and leads eventually to destruction. To surrender to Jesus is to be offered "life more abundant" and eternal. I am determined to choose that abundant, better, higher, selfless, more fruitful life. Which do you choose?

Write or email me and let me know if you also hunger and thirst for that greater life. More importantly let Jesus know. Begin now to be putty in His hands. Give up your ways for His, your thoughts for His. Make the rest of your life count for things eternal. Don't expect it to be easy. There is a great spiritual war raging. Are you engaged in it? It can cost you. Jesus in Matthew 10 gives a vivid description of what it costs to follow Him. He sums it up with "And he who does not take his cross and follow after Me is not worthy of Me. He who finds his life will lose it, and he who loses his life for My sake will find it" Matt 10:38, 39. Whose pleasure do you intend to live in? God's? Yours? Man's? Satan's? "Choose this day who you will serve, as for me and my house, we will serve the Lord." I hope you, like me, made the decision to let Jesus walk "In My Steps."

Feel free to contact me and tell me how you were blessed by reading the story of Jesus "In My Steps." I would love to hear what Jesus has done for you. He is on the horizon. He is coming. His return is sure and certain. It will be soon and that will be:

THE BEGINNING

pneuma123@yahoo.com

POST SCRIPT

As we were doing the final editing before submitting this manuscript to the publisher another great tragedy hit this nation. 20 children and 6 adults were violently murdered in Sandy Hook elementary school in Newtown, Connecticut. At the same time another outbreak of evil took place in China where an evil driven man killed as many children with a knife. Our world is shaken and perplexed with such atrocities. Terrorism abounds and spreads throughout the world. Wars rage. Towers tumble. Millions of babies die at the hand of heartless men and women in abortion clinics. The abominable evil of homosexuality spreads in our society like cancer. Truth falls in the courts and political halls of our nation. God is crowded out. The Ten Commandments are mocked and removed from public places. Nativity scenes are ripped from the court house lawns. Bibles and prayer and any mention of God are forbidden in the class-rooms. Jesus Christ has become more of a swear word rather than a prayer word. Where light is extinguished darkness moves in and prevails. Where truth is mocked and subdued, lies and deceptions take root and rule. And it always ends in violence and terrorism.

Jesus warned of these days as the end draws near "and because lawlessness will abound, the love of many will grow cold" Matt. 24:12. He warned that the tribulation of these final days would be so bad "unless those days were shortened no flesh would be saved; but for the elect's sake those days will be shortened" vs. 22. The Apostle Paul warned of these days "But know this, that in the last days perilous times will come: for men will be lovers of themselves, lovers of money, boasters, proud, blasphemers, disobedient to parents, unthankful, unholy, unloving, unforgiving, slanderers, without self-control, brutal, despisers of good, traitors, headstrong, haughty, lovers of pleasure rather that lovers of God, having a form of godliness but denying its power" 2 Timothy 3:1-5. What a vivid description of the evil invading society in these last days. Again we are warned in Revelation 12:12 "Woe to the inhabitants of the earth and the sea! For the devil has come down to you, having great wrath, because he knows that he has a short time." One of his greatest deceptions is persuading people that he does not exist, yet the truth is that "he is enraged" and has gone out "to make war with those who keep the commandments of God and have the testimony of Jesus Christ" Revelation 12:17.

Jesus warned this "thief does not come except to steal, and to kill, and to destroy. I have come that they may have life, and that they may have it more abundantly" John 10:10. As sure as a duck goes to water so is Satan and his demons driven to steal, kill and destroy. Killing babies is second nature to him. From the beginning he lied to and deceived Eve and he has never backed down. Peter warned us "Be sober, be vigilant because your adversary the devil walks about like a roaring lion, seeking whom he may devour. Resist him steadfast in the faith, knowing that the same sufferings are experienced by your brotherhood in the world." He is everywhere with his hordes of fallen angels. Those who deny his existence are the more accessible to his evil wiles. Destruction will follow wherever he gets a foot-hold. Millions of unborn babies have suffered murder at his insidious incentives. Dozens of little children have died before the rage of an evil-crazed man; not only in our class-rooms, but in our homes where parents have lost connection with God and yielded to the creeping presence of this dark evil kingdom. It is only going to get worse.

"Where is God?" people are asking. "What can be done?" You will not find the answers in more government control and more stringent laws. You won't find the answers in our schools of higher, elite education. You won't find solutions in the staid, traditional, self-righteous, man-made churches. The answer is in YOU dear believer. Jesus said "YOU are the salt of the earth" and "YOU are the light of the world" Matt 5:13, 14. You have no idea what power you possess as a believer in Jesus Christ. You can make real changes. James 5:16 says "The effective, fervent prayer of a righteous man avails much." "Avails much" means it "accomplishes a lot." There is a power within you waiting to be released. "Now to Him who is able to do exceedingly abundantly above all that we ask or think, according to the power that works in us, to Him be glory in the church by Christ Jesus to all generations, forever and ever. Amen" Eph. 3:20, 21. God's people have not begun to draw on the power, strength and authority given to them. The call has echoed through the centuries to the people called by His name: "If My people who are called by My name will humble themselves, and pray and seek My face, and turn from their wicked ways, then I will hear from heaven, and will forgive their sin and heal their land" 2 Chron. 7:14. Jesus said "I give you the authority to trample on serpents and scorpions, and over all the power of the enemy" Luke 10:19. The truth is that we are in a great war against evil. Paul exhorts us "Finally my brethren, be strong in the Lord and in the power of His might. Put on the whole armor of God, that you may be able to stand against the wiles of the devil, for we do not wrestle against flesh and blood, but against principalities, against powers, against the rulers of darkness of this age, against spiritual hosts of wickedness in the heavenly places" Eph. 6:10-12.

Where is God? He is in you, waiting to be released. Jesus wants to live His life in you to bring light, life and love into this dark evil world. We need to experience what Paul testifies in Gal. 2:20 "I have been crucified with Christ it is no longer I who live, but Christ lives in me." We need to echo his driving ambition in Phil 1:20 it is "my earnest expectation and hope that in nothing I shall be ashamed, but with all boldness, as always, so now also Christ will be magnified in my body, whether by life or by death." Jesus Christ living in you is the "hope of glory." He wants to walk in your feet, work with your hands, love through your heart, think with your mind, speak with your mouth. That is the great dynamic of the Christian life that I've tried to share with you in this book. You see the great need of it in our evil-wracked world. It's past time to quit playing church and religious games and get real with the truth. You can let Jesus live in you. Together we can experience going boldly where no man has ever gone before. Quit following the patterns of those around you. Dare to step into the arena of being light and salt. Learn to lose your life in order to gain His. God calls us to decrease so Jesus can increase. He calls us to die so Jesus can live. Will you be part of that answer? Are you willing to say "I want Jesus to walk In My Steps?" Begin now to seek and call on Him to that end.

A SECOND POSTSCRIPT

While this book is being processed in the hands of my publisher I discovered I have stage four cancer. At this point I do not know exactly how bad it is, but it does not sound good. The adventure with Jesus continues. I know He is King of cancer, whether by life or by death.

I have pondered Job's trials, his loss of kids, crops, cattle and later his deteriorated health and lack of support from his three best friends. In the end Job discovered God is King over kids, crops, cattle and character. All his losses were doubled back in blessings to him. Likewise Joseph suffered great evil by the hand of his hateful brothers and the wicked wife of Potiphar. Like Job, in the end Joseph discovered God is King over mean brothers and wild women. He was exalted as a wise and powerful governor in Egypt second only to the Pharaoh. In his exalted position he brought salvation from starvation and the preservation of his family from devastation.

In my case God is making cancer another step in the adventure of Jesus walking "In My Steps." It might turn out not as something doubled back in my life, but something quadruped in the lives of my children, grandchildren, great grandchildren and even the two great great grandchildren. As I write this a great grand-child is making plans and raising funds for another mission trip to Africa. Go Kayya! Another great grand-daughter, grand-daughter and a grandson are all furthering their education in college. Go Kassie, Tabby, and Jacob! Perhaps not in me, but in my 50 member family you will see God's ongoing ability to turn evil into good. Maybe the next book will be by one of them telling you how they discovered Jesus walking "In My Steps." Let the future unfold. The adventure continues. Go family!

I must testify that the threat of death has greatly enhanced my faith. Things I have believed before I now believe with more confidence than ever. My joy has increased to that "joy unspeakable and full of glory." My peace has deepened to that "peace that passes understanding." My love for God, family and fellow man has blossomed to unlimited expanses. My hope has brightened to where I have keen expectation with certainty that I shall again see my mother, brother, son-in-law, old mentor (no longer old), those precious little ones that died in the womb and all loved ones that have preceded me beyond the veil. If it takes cancer to so sharpen my spiritual senses, I can only say bring it on. Let the adventure continue. Hallelujah.

ACKNOWLEDGEMENTS

It's always difficult to list acknowledgements. There are many who have encouraged me, helped me and prayed for the production of this book. Over 40 years ago the late Floyd Kelly, elder at Westside church, prophesied: "Someday you will write a book titled 'In My Steps.'" He didn't live here to see it, but surely enjoys it from the view of our future home.

I appreciate all the prayers and encouragement from my 50 member family, and from many dear friends. A special thanks to all the helpful staff at Abbott Press, especially Donavon, John, Eric, Shawn and Amanda who helped bring this book to reality.

Above all I appreciate and acknowledge the One who walks "In My Steps" without who this book would have no meaning or even be possible. Thank you Jesus.